COPING WITH

Eating

Disorders

Barbara Moe

THE ROSEN PUBLISHING GROUP, INC./NEW YORK

Published in 1991, 1995 by The Rosen Publishing Group, Inc.
29 East 21st Street, New York, NY 10010

Revised Edition 1995

Library of Congress Cataloging-in-Publication Data

Moe, Barbara A.
  Coping with eating disorders/Barbara Moe.—rev. ed.
      p.   cm.
  Includes bibliographical references and index.
    Summary: Describes the different kinds of eating disorders, what can cause them, and what can be done about them.
  ISBN 0-8239-2133-6
    1. Eating disorders—Juvenile literature.   [1. Eating disorders.]
  I. Title
  RC552.E18M64   1991
  616.85'26—dc20

Manufactured in the United States of America

ABOUT THE AUTHOR

B arbara Moe has a Bachelor of Science degree in Nursing from the College of Nursing and Health, University of Cincinnati, and a master of Science degree in Nursing from Ohio State University. She received her Master of Social Work degree, as well as a Certificate of Marriage and Family Therapy, from the University of Denver.

Contents

Prologue iv

1 Surveying the Scene 1

2 The Media's Message 19

3 Ladies First? Women in Today's Society 27

4 Families 38

5 Feeling Your Feelings 55

6 The Road to Maturity 69

7 Eating Well/Living Well 82

8 Everything Else You've Always Wanted to Know . . . 88

9 Getting Better 103

10 Recognizing an Eating Disorder 126

11 Prevention 132

12 Resources 136

Epilogue 140

Glossary 141

For Further Reading 142

Index 145

Prologue

A worried parent writes to her daughter, Liz, attending college two hours from home:

"Dearest Liz:

I'm so concerned about you. You look too thin, emaciated, unhealthy, and unhappy. Your diet doesn't seem adequate for a bird. When we saw you last week, I noticed the sores at the corners of your mouth. I've heard you complain about dry skin and cracks on your hands and feet. Those things are no doubt the result of nutritional deficiency. Add to that the depression, lack of energy, moodiness, and angry outbursts.

I'm scared. I'm afraid you're on the verge of *serious* health problems. Therefore, I'm going to give you a choice of options:

1. You can find a therapist on your own. Maybe you could ask the school to recommend one who specializes in eating disorders.
2. We can all go to a therapist together.
3. You can be hospitalized (examined, monitored, possibly force-fed through a tube into your stomach or intravenously) until your health returns.

In a week I need to know which of the above you've chosen. If you choose the first or second option, you also need to have a physical exam, as you promised to do six months ago.

I love you *very* much and certainly have no desire to outlive my oldest daughter.

Much love,
Mom

CHAPTER ◇ 1

Surveying the Scene

Liz: Not Good Enough

She has long, blonde hair and hazel eyes; heads turn as she walks by. Liz lives in a suburb of a large California city. Her father, a business executive, and her mother, a volunteer worker, have been married twenty-five years. Liz has a brother, Tim, nineteen, and a sister, Jenny, fourteen. For some reason she can't explain, Liz has never felt "good enough."

Liz calls her mother a "fitness freak." Mom swims every day and goes to an aerobics class on Saturdays. On Sundays she relaxes by taking a long bike ride. Liz's father is involved in his work.

When Liz was about seventeen, the eating problems began. She had gone to her favorite summer camp as an assistant counselor. One night the regular counselors went to a meeting in the lodge. They left Liz in charge of a cabin full of eleven-year-olds. The kids started getting wild. Liz threatened to tell.

Angry at her, one of the campers said, "You big ole butt!"

Liz took the camper's words seriously. Although she

1

wasn't really overweight, she began to feel fat. By the time Liz went home at the end of that summer, she had lost seventeen pounds. Her weight loss produced positive comments from her family members, who thought she looked great. "Just like a model," said her older brother with an appreciative smile.

Still, Liz thought she looked too fat. Even though she was hungry all the time, she didn't want to eat. She avoided family meals by saying she'd had a late lunch or a big snack after school. If she *had* to eat with the family, she helped herself to mounds of lettuce and chewed each bite twenty times before swallowing. Then she washed down the lettuce with several glasses of ice water.

Every morning before school, Liz jogged five miles. At first she felt great. For once she felt in control of her life. No matter how hard they begged, Liz's family could not change her goal of getting thinner.

Liz's mother panicked one day when she saw Liz without the bulky sweatshirt she always wore. Her daughter looked like a skeleton. Liz still thought she looked fat. She pinched the loose, dry skin at the top of her wrists and said, "See, I'm fat! I'm fat!"

A few days later, Liz's mom took her to the family doctor. He told Liz she had a slight case of anorexia, and she had better start eating.

That night the family had spaghetti, one of Liz's favorite meals. The dinner conversation had something to do with the Browns, the family across the street, who had kids of similar ages. The Brown children did this; the Brown children did that. Liz got the idea. The Brown children were better in every way. She'd had that feeling her whole life. She wished she had clear goals and an adventurous spirit like the Brown children. She wished she knew the right way to live.

Liz pushed the pasta around on her plate, but she took only a bite or two. And yet she felt full—uncomfortable. She could hardly wait to go up to the bathroom. Maybe she'd throw up.

By the time she got to college, Liz was still wrestling with her life choices—and with her eating disorder. Here is an excerpt from her diary:

"I think so much of my parents' opinions on things, and I can't help letting their ideas influence mine. On the other hand, I have to make up my own mind about things—my life, my job (career), etc. There seem to be more decisions now than at any other time in a person's life. Whether or not to have one boyfriend or choose to meet lots of people, picking a major, staying in school or working, how to make money, where to live, etc. And to be constantly worried about your weight, and your life, and if what you're doing with your life is right—or enough. Darn! I never feel as if I'm doing enough or *can* do enough."

About this time, Liz's mother wrote the letter in the Prologue. Liz definitely had an eating problem, and she shared many of the characteristics common to those with anorexia, bulimia, compulsive eating, and exercise disorders.

Why?

According to ANRED, an organization listed at the end of this book, "As bizarre as they seem, these disorders are easy to understand. Starving, stuffing, purging, and compulsive exercising are nothing more than coping behaviors—people's best attempts to solve problems and meet their needs. . . . If they want to recover, they must find healthier ways of managing their lives."

Ladies (and Men) of the Nineties

People of the nineties want to be thin and physically fit. They seem to be trying to obey the media's messages: "Be skinny. If you are thin, you will be gorgeous, fun-to-be-with, sexy, healthy, and accepted wherever you go. All your problems will be solved." Perhaps as the result of listening to such messages:

- Eight million Americans suffer from anorexia nervosa and bulimia nervosa.
- Some researchers estimate that half of those with anorexia eventually become bulimic.
- Approximately 80 percent of girls under the age of thirteen say they have already tried dieting.
- Dieting is one of the most common triggers for anorexia and bulimia.

Myths and Facts About Eating Disorders

Myth: Victims of eating disorders are either middle- or upper-class white people.

Fact: It is true that eating disorders are often seen in high-income, highly educated groups of people, but research shows that no group is immune. Experts propose at least two reasons: (1) because of wide exposure to the mass media, people of all races and social classes have acquired similar notions about the ideal body image; and (2) many people are becoming familiar with the disorders and are therefore more willing to seek help than in the past. Specialists in eating disorders work with women (and men) of all colors and classes. People struggling with basic survival needs, however, are unlikely to develop eating disorders. We see them only in countries where food is relatively plentiful. Writer and dancer Maya Browne wrote in *Essence* (June 1993), "Most people believe that Black folks don't suffer from eating disorders. That it's a white thing. But the truth is that a growing number of Black women are living in the secret and dangerous worlds of anorexia and bulimia."

Myth: Only teenagers get eating disorders.

Fact: Although adolescence is the prime time for the development of an eating disorder, the teenage years are not the only time. Cases of anorexia nervosa and bulimia seem to be starting earlier. Doctors have seen anorexia in children as young as eight years, but twelve is the average age. Eighteen is the average age for bulimia to begin. Many people report they know of an older relative with an eating problem. One sixty-year-old woman called her doctor after reading an article about bulimia. She had suffered with the condition for thirty years and had always considered herself a freak.

Myth: Eating disorders affect only females.

Fact: Although most people who seek treatment for anorexia or bulimia are female, males get eating disorders too. Authorities estimate that between 5 and 10 percent of persons with eating disorders are male; the numbers are rising. Current estimates put the number of males with eating disorders around one million. Many of these boys and men are involved in sports such as wrestling and gymnastics in which weight is a factor. Jockeys, models, and actors are also at risk. So are gay men or those who are confused about their sexual orientation. Males usually develop eating disorders in late adolescence or in the early twenties.

Males with eating disorders have an even greater problem than females; they are thought to have a "woman's disease." Therefore, more males than females may be hiding their difficulties. Some marathon runners, for example, may be anorexics in disguise. But because the majority of cases (at least those reported) occur in females, books on the subject most often use the pronoun "she" when referring to someone with an eating disorder.

Addiction: A Short-Term Fix

Many factors contribute to eating disorders. Eating disorders have less to do with food and more to do with low self-esteem, depression, troubles with intimacy, problems with control, and dealings with society's expectations. Considering eating disorders as addictive behaviors makes some experts unhappy, but it helps others to understand and treat their clients.

One authority has described eating disorders as "obsession with weight and addiction to food." Of course, the person with an eating disorder is not really addicted to food itself. In fact, we could say that anorexics are addicted to *avoiding* food and to being thin.

The addictive element is more complicated in bulimia. Many bulimics say they are addicted to feeling numb, which is the state they're in while stuffing themselves. Some are addicted to the comfort they receive from the predictability of the binge-purge cycle. They may have come from chaotic homes where not much has ever been predictable. Experts believe that those who have a close relative who is alcoholic may have more of a tendency to develop bulimia. Others say that close to 50 percent of those with bulimia have suffered from abuse or incest in childhood.

There is also much that studies do not show. For example, some young people have suffered from emotional abuse so hidden that neither the parents nor their children are aware of it. Parents who are unable to meet their children's emotional needs may not know they're abusing their children; they may think of it only as neglect.

Having an eating disorder is the way some people avoid dealing with painful feelings. After all, when a person's thoughts are constantly of food, little room is left for painful thoughts.

Medical experts remind us that not all addictions are similar. Cocaine, nicotine, and alcohol can create a physical dependency. That kind of drug dependency is different from compulsive eating.

Nevertheless, a *kind* of addiction is certainly part of the eating disorder picture. Perhaps we should use the word "habit" or "compulsion." In any case, most people who started these behaviors thought they could stop them at any time. They found out they were wrong.

A family therapist, Claudia Bepko, says that because our society is based on male dominance, female addictions are different from male addictions. "For males, money, sexuality, size, strength, and competitive work convey power and status. Consequently, gambling, sexual addictions, and workaholism tend to be predominantly male forms of compulsive behavior. Women are socialized to concern themselves with physical and emotional nurturing, so that eating disorders, obsessive shopping or cleaning, and compulsive behaviors in relationships are common female forms of addictive behavior." Binge-purge parties in college dormitories and sorority houses are not uncommon.

Roommates: Partners in Food

The sorority sisters didn't send out invitations to this binge-purge party. The situation developed informally. Roommates Erica and Marcie loved to eat. What they didn't love to eat was the gross tuna-noodle casserole that appeared on the table Thursday evening. After a little eating followed by serious studying, they felt in need of some nurturing. They invited Barbie and Rita to join them on a walk to a nearby convenience store. They each bought three of their favorite junk-food items.

Back in the room, they shared the food. They washed down the Twinkies with Kahlua and cream. Later they all felt sick. Marcie, Barbie, and Rita went to bed to sleep it off. Erica went into the bathroom and vomited.

Many people need only one such experience to have had enough. Others can't quit.

Jane never participated in a binge-purge party in college. She did her bingeing in private. "I never felt good after a binge—I felt awful. My stomach hurt and pooched out, and then I'd go to the mirror to look at my big fat thighs that touched in the middle. After I threw up, I felt hopeful for a short time. But as soon as I finished the binge, I had to sleep. Each time I prayed tomorrow would be different. Yet when I woke up, I began planning for the next binge. What a waste of time."

In summary we can say that an addiction or compulsion exists when a person is no longer able to make choices about his or her behavior. Jane's report shows that a person's obsession with food can be a short-term fix for a long-term problem. The trouble is that the fix (food) is not a fix—and it may not be short term.

ANOREXIA NERVOSA

Anorexia nervosa is often called anorexia for short. Anorexia means "loss of appetite," but most people with the condition are hungry all the time. In fact, because they eat so little, they are absolutely preoccupied with thoughts of food. They are starving themselves, sometimes to death.

Anorexia is a group of thoughts and behaviors that includes:

- fear of getting fat (although the person is underweight);
- refusal to maintain a body weight that is minimum normal for age and height;
- disturbance of body image (feeling fat despite looking emaciated); and
- stopping of menstrual periods for three consecutive cycles (or never starting them) when there is no other reason for their absence. In males the presence of the first three signs would make one wonder about anorexia.

Although there is no single personality type, people who develop anorexia tend to share certain characteristics. Their parents often describe them as model children, high achievers who have never given an ounce of trouble. They are perfectionists; they tend to be self-critical. They also tend to be very controlled people who stick to schedules and don't like changes in routine. An anorexic may not consciously realize that her behavior is making a statement about what is wrong in her family, but sometimes that is the case. For example, disturbed communication patterns in a family and anorexia nervosa may go hand in hand. In the doctor's office Mom may always answer for her daughter; no wonder Daughter feels as if she lacks control.

Anorexia sometimes begins with a simple diet and progresses to a power struggle over weight and food. The person uses eating as a way of controlling those close to her. Self-denial makes her feel virtuous and powerful. Nothing gives her so much pleasure as dieting and losing weight. She loves hearing people tell her how thin she looks.

Because anorexia most often shows up around puberty, some theorize that anorexics are afraid of intimacy, sexuality, and the responsibilities of adulthood. A girl may be angry at the demands society places on her.

Sheila: A Broomstick

Sheila, twenty-eight, denies that she was ever anorexic. But Sheila's mother remembers how her daughter looked in high school plays. "She was five feet seven and weighed 104 pounds. She looked like a broomstick dancing around on stage." Sheila's mother also has a theory about the event that triggered her daughter's eating disorder. "She was in sixth grade. We were having dinner one night, and her father made a remark he considered funny. 'Sheila,' he said, 'it looks as if you're starting to grow boobs as nice as your mother's.' At that Sheila's face flushed. She stood up and threw her plate at her father. Not long after that she started finding excuses not to eat with us."

*   *   *

Many times a more stressful event than Sheila's confrontation with her father precedes anorexia or bulimia. Sheila's parents were having marital difficulties at the time and eventually divorced. Common triggers of eating disorders are parental divorce, a death in the family, illness, loss of a boyfriend or girlfriend, a family move, a change of schools, or starting college.

Bill: A Male Anorexic

Bill was twelve when he came down with a bad case of the flu. For several days afterward he didn't have much appetite. He enjoyed feeling "lean and mean" like the long-distance runners he read about in the sports pages. At the same time his older sister squeezed his waist and said, "Hey, you better quit eating so many ice cream bars. You're getting a spare tire just like Dad."

The next day for breakfast Bill allowed himself six raisins. He had a raw carrot for lunch. After school he came home and did sit-ups and push-ups on a schedule he'd made for himself. Bill kept up this routine of starving and exercising for about ten days.

Finally he got so hungry he blew his control and made a huge grilled meat and cheese sandwich, which he thoroughly enjoyed. After that he decided to drop his rigid diet and exercise program. It didn't seem worth the suffering. "Maybe," he says, "I gave it up because Mom exploded when she found that exercise list under my bed."

Experts don't know what enables a person like Bill to stop self-destructive behavior whereas another person (like Liz) carries it on for years. Why do some people develop eating disorders as a way of dealing with family problems or painful feelings? Later we'll explore some possible reasons.

BULIMIA NERVOSA

Bulimia nervosa, an eating disorder related to anorexia nervosa, is usually called bulimia. The word *bulimia* means "ox-hunger" in Greek and is a medical term for binge eating or gorging. But the victims of the condition are hungry for more than food. They are hungry for love, approval, and acceptance. Attempting to please everyone around her, the bulimic often pleases no one, including herself. When faced with life choices, she may not be able to make a choice. Instead, she may act impulsively and get involved in shoplifting, in excessive use of alcohol or drugs, or in undesirable relationships with men. In fact, bulimics often use men to try to validate their self-worth, which they measure in terms of achievement or outward appearances.

Bulimics may be underweight, overweight, or of normal weight. A person with bulimia often "binges" (eats a large amount of food in a short time) and feels that she can't stop even if she wants to. After the binge she feels guilty and depressed. Like the person with anorexia, she is overconcerned with her body weight and shape. And also like the anorexic, she may try to get rid of unwanted calories by excessive exercise. To keep from gaining weight, she may "purge" by making herself vomit or by using laxatives or diuretics (pills that increase urine output). Sometimes after a binge she can do nothing but sleep. Or she may decide to start a strict diet—tomorrow.

Back as a camp counselor in her eighteenth year, Liz kept up her diary: "Tonight some of us went to town to buy groceries. Of course I bought a bag of gorp. I've been living on junk food. I've eaten a lot at night after everyone else is asleep. I hoard all this stuff—mostly chips and candy bars."

Bulimics tend to have other characteristics in common. They usually have low self-esteem (a poor opinion of themselves) and trouble expressing their feelings. They use bingeing and purging as a way of dealing with stress or negative feelings. Sometimes they dissociate from their feelings; they are not in touch with them. They don't know how they feel. Many bulimics have inadequate coping skills. For example, being assertive or expressing anger may be hard for them. Vomiting may be one way (an unhealthy way, to be sure) of trying to express anger. In some people, a stressful life event may trigger a binge. Because bulimia tends to start later in life than anorexia, the stressful event is often separation from home, such as going away to college.

When Liz came home from camp the first year, her mother had no idea what was wrong with her daughter. She only knew that Liz's behavior was driving both of them crazy. She complained to the doctor: "Liz says she has terrible pains in her stomach. No wonder! She chews gum and drinks coffee constantly—even when I tell her to stop. She acts like a two-year-old the way she dribbles granola and cake crumbs all over the house. It feels like hostility directed at me."

Meanwhile Liz's earlier anorexia had evolved into bulimia. She wrote: "All of the other counselors know about my eating problem. Tonight I heard the nurse talking about me. At the time, I happened to be in the kitchen sneaking food. I ran to hide in the bathroom in the hall. I could hear several of them talking and giggling. I stayed in the bathroom about forty-five minutes. Finally

I slammed the back door and went crying to my cabin. Oh, God, help me! I hate being FAT and unhappy."

People with anorexia and bulimia may have traits in common, but they have at least one major difference. Anorexics are usually secretly proud of their self-starvation because of the feeling of control it gives them. Bulimics, on the other hand, feel ashamed and out of control. They may try to hide evidence of binges, or they may (as a cry for help?) leave evidence of binges around the house. Sometimes getting the secret out in the open can start the healing process.

COMPULSIVE EATING:
BINGE EATING DISORDER (BED)

Let's face it. Most of us have used food as a pacifier. Comfort food can soothe wounded feelings or provide strength for a tough task ahead. "I *need* some fries." "I *have* to have a hot fudge sundae." That's okay, say most experts, unless you get into a habit of emotional eating that makes you feel bad about yourself.

According to the dictionary, a compulsion is "an irresistible impulse to act, regardless of the rationality of the motivation." A compulsion is unthinking and automatic. People put themselves on automatic pilot when they don't know how to feel their feelings or don't want to.

Binge eating disorder is a relatively new name for the category of eating disorders sometimes called compulsive eating or compulsive overeating. Older women, such as media superstar Oprah Winfrey, are more likely than younger people to have this condition. However, some experts estimate that BED affects as many as 4 percent of college-age women.

A compulsive eater or overeater is someone who eats even when not hungry. The person may eat impulsively or almost continuously. Compulsive eating is out-of-control eating. Although the compulsive eater realizes that her behavior is abnormal, she seems powerless to stop it. Unlike the bulimic person, the compulsive eater doesn't try to purge by vomiting or using laxatives. But, like the person with bulimia, the compulsive eater feels depressed after a binge. She may be overweight and go on a diet so strict it sets her up to binge all over again. Vicki, for example, eats nothing all day. By evening she's like a wild animal, sinking her teeth into anything edible. Sometimes she's like a boa constrictor, swallowing her food whole. The next morning she still feels stuffed. She eats no breakfast or lunch, and the cycle repeats itself. Like anorexia and bulimia, compulsive eating is a response to emotional pain, a dysfunctional way of trying to deal with the stress and conflicts of life.

Caitlin: The Grazer

"I became aware that I was a compulsive overeater two and a half years ago. I was reading a book by a therapist, who described crossing the line from normal eating to food addiction. Since my child was born, I had been struggling with food and overeating more than ever before, and I was home a lot. I knew I had crossed the line when I had a normal breakfast, then kept eating or grazing until lunchtime. Then I ate lunch! It's not that I ate whole cakes or pies, but that I snacked on little bits continuously. I felt out of control and somewhat dazed. I was tired, lonely, and angry."

Compulsive eaters may share one or more of several other characteristics. Like Caitlin they may feel tired all the time, have mood swings, develop high blood pressure, and experience swelling and bloating. They may also be victims of the "yo-yo" syndrome, which refers to extremes of weight fluctuation.

Anorexia, bulimia, and binge eating disorder are the extremes of eating disorders. But many young people suffer from disordered eating practices, such as the use of fad diets; the abuse of laxatives, diuretics, and diet pills; and compulsive exercise.

COMPULSIVE EXERCISE

We all know that exercise is part of a healthy lifestyle. But some people don't know when to quit. Compulsive exercisers have an irresistible impulse to exercise; they feel uncomfortable and anxious when not working out.

These people may exercise every day for several hours. They don't look at exercise as something to enjoy; they consider it a job to get done. The trouble is that the job never gets finished. Compulsive exercisers may ignore friends, school, or work in pursuit of their goal. They may also have disordered eating (problems with weight and food). Compulsive exercise can cause torn ligaments and cartilage as well as broken bones.

The Female Athlete Triad

Three features of disordered eating and exercising in women athletes can cause an especially dangerous situation: First, an eating disorder that excludes certain nutrients from the diet; second, stopping of menstruation or missing several periods because of starvation and excessive exercise;

and third, early osteoporosis, causing broken bones. (Osteoporosis is loss of bone mass and bone minerals that usually occurs in much older people.) Experts say that when the person gains some weight, reduces exercise intensity, and has menstrual periods again, bone density may come back. In other cases the damage may *not* be reversible.

Some male and female athletes hope to increase their athletic abilities by shrinking their size; however, the opposite may occur and athletic performance decreases.

Samantha: Hurting

To her family's surprise, Samantha became a cross-country runner in her first year of college. Her parents were further amazed by her rapid weight loss—eighteen pounds during her first semester. When she came home for the December holidays, she complained of a sore leg. Her doctor discovered a stress fracture. Samantha had the female athlete triad.

Where Are We Heading?

The late Dr. Hilde Bruch, an eating disorder specialist for forty years, saw a change over time in the pattern of eating disorders. Most of the anorexic patients she saw in the fifties and sixties showed similarities. And yet it was as if each patient had never heard of the condition before she developed her own disorder. In the seventies and eighties, however, changes took place. Most of those with eating disorders knew someone who had a similar condition. As we have seen, eating disorders are common on college campuses. Bulimia often seems like a contagious disease with one person catching (i.e., learning) it from someone else.

Another trend may be a decrease in the number of *severe* cases of anorexia while less severe, but still disordered, eating habits increase. One thing all eating disorders have in common is their link to emotional pain.

CHAPTER 2

The Media's Message

D o you believe everything you see on TV? Of course not. But how about newspapers, magazines, and movies? No one can say for sure that the media are responsible for the tremendous increase in the number of cases of eating disorders over the past several years, but the media have certainly had an influence.

What do we mean by "the media"? Films, television, newspapers, magazines, books, CDs, tapes, radio, billboards. They bombard us with messages we sometimes accept without thinking.

Rhonda: Rejection!

Rhonda remembers the day she decided to go on a diet. She had just turned sixteen and had gotten a ride home from school with one of her friends who already had her driver's license.

Rhonda's parents wouldn't let her take driver's ed yet; they said she was too young and insisted on taking her back and forth every weekend to her job at Rosa's Tortilla Palace.

Rhonda had had a hard day at school. That morning she had summoned up her courage and invited Brad Byerly to the Sadie Hawkins dance. "I was wondering if you'd be free . . ." she had mumbled. "You know, the dance." He had given her one of his gorgeous toothy smiles and said, "Well, I'd like to, but I have to go to my grandmother's that weekend."

Today in last period, Rhonda had heard that Mary Jensen had asked him. And what had he said? "Sure, Mary, I'd love to go."

When she got home, Rhonda needed a little TV to "numb out." She caught the end of her favorite soap. One commercial showed a tall, slim blonde, who looked like Mary Jensen, sitting across a tiny outdoor table from a handsome guy, who resembled Brad Byerly. The girl picked at her salad while she held the guy's hand under the table. "You too can get your man," said the TV voice. "Just be sure to use Ida's Low Cal Italian Dressing."

That night Rhonda announced her plan to diet. Her mother, who had always considered Rhonda a bit chunky and who was on a perpetual diet herself, didn't protest. The next day when Rhonda arrived home from school, she found a huge bowl of raw veggies in the refrigerator. Over the next few weeks, low-cal dinners appeared. Whenever the supply of lettuce, celery, and carrots dwindled, Rhonda's mother dashed to the store to replenish them.

That was the beginning of a thirty-pound weight loss for Rhonda. She became anorexic. A few months later she became bulimic. Her starvation diet had made her ravenously hungry; it seemed she couldn't get enough to eat. After starving herself all day, she binged half the night on cookies, potato chips, and chocolates she hid under the bed.

Much later in a family therapy session, Rhonda's mother

revealed her feelings of guilt over having encouraged her daughter to diet. Perhaps another reason for Rhonda's problems was her parents' overprotection; they had not allowed their daughter to make enough of her own decisions. As a result her self-esteem was low.

Neither Rhonda's parents nor the television commercials were the total cause of Rhonda's eating disorder; many factors played a part. We all see and hear thinness messages daily. Although we can't draw definite conclusions about what causes what, we can examine the facts.

What Do You See on TV?

More than ten years ago Dr. John Murray published research on television viewing. He studied nearly three thousand published works to find out the following:

- Many children watch at least four hours of TV every day.
- By the time these children get to high school, they will have watched fifteen thousand hours of TV compared to the eleven thousand hours they have spent in school.
- They will have seen 350,000 commercials, more than half of which were for food.

Other researchers have studied body types on television. They found that close to 90 percent of TV characters are thin or average in body build. Television tends to make fun of fat people. And yet television viewing itself seems to promote obesity. Teens who watch a lot of TV weigh more than the average young person.

We all know that television has a big influence on our lives. One study predicted that most viewers see more than five thousand attractiveness commercials each year. Half of these commercials emphasize the importance of physical beauty.

Many young people believe what they see on TV; they accept television as reality. Some eating disorder specialists call today's teens "the Weight Watcher generation." Teenagers may believe that their happiness depends on achieving the perfect body they see on TV.

People in the United States spend at least $30 billion each year on physical fitness and weight-loss materials. They spend $10 billion on diet soft drinks alone.

Even our comic strip characters are obsessed with food. Everyone's favorite cat Garfield is definitely preoccupied. Can Garfield help it if he wants to dine at "Ernie's Eat Till You Explode Restaurant"? After all, he's just a cat.

Advertising: Mind Control?

Several years ago the United States Institute of Advertising prepared a special report entitled *Best Fitness/Weight Loss Advertising*. The examples were taken from more than eight hundred Sunday newspapers and other print media. Advertisers try to "direct" their ads—like an arrow to a bull's-eye—to a specific audience. One of the six groups at whom the advertisers aim their "arrows" are "new consumers; first buyers, usually the younger . . . They respond to the most appealing message." Pictures of women dominate almost all of the winning advertisements. "Readers relate to illustrations showing other people like themselves," says the report, "or people they wish they were like."

More Media

Boys often identify with physical strength in TV characters; girls most often identify with physical attractiveness (e.g., slimness). In many television programs and advertisements, thin people get ahead while fat people get laughed at.

The media blitz us with information about the hazards of being overweight. Studies have shown, however, that being a little overweight is *not* a health hazard. On the other hand, as we have seen, being too thin *can* be a hazard to health. For example, girls who are afraid of getting fat may get little calcium during adolescence. Then they are at great risk later in life for developing osteoporosis, the disease of brittle bones.

Our Heroes and Heroines

Eating disorders victimize some of the same media personalities that young women (and men) admire. We know that dancers, actresses, and fashion models are at high risk for eating disorders. Their jobs demand thinness. Jane Fonda's bulimia lasted twenty-three years, from age twelve to age thirty-five. In *Citizen Jane: The Turbulent Life of Jane Fonda*, Christopher Anderson writes, "By her junior year, Jane hit upon a way to shed unsightly pounds. After dinner, she would go to the bathroom, turn on the tap so no one could hear, then stick her finger down her throat to induce vomiting. Thus, in 1945, long before everyone knew the word bulimia, Jane began the dangerous binge-and-purge cycle that would continue for another 'twenty-three years of agony.'"

In her book *Starving for Affection*, Cherry Boone O'Neill, the oldest daughter of a famous recording star, tells of her need to be perfect and of the strict diet she imposed on herself, beginning at age thirteen. "Straight As were my uncompromising objective. I knew I was capable of them, and I wouldn't settle for less. In the fourth grade I would stay up until eleven o'clock to put the finishing touches on my homework. The mere thought of falling below my personal scholastic standards flooded me with panic."

Recording star Karen Carpenter died from complications of an eating disorder. In *People* (November 2, 1983), her brother remembers: "Karen was always worried about the way she looked, so I tried to appeal to that. I told her she was too thin and that people were noticing it. And that she wouldn't be able to continue our schedule if she didn't get more fuel. Although her voice was never affected, you could hear gasps from the audience when she came on stage, and there was considerable mail from fans asking what was wrong. Eventually, though, my parents and I realized that there was nothing we could do except state what was on our minds. We never knew how to help her."

Jill: The People-Pleaser

Jill is not a media personality nor a Miss America contestant, but she's a "star" to the members of her family. They didn't mind that she failed to get the internship she wanted at a local television station. But Jill cared. She decided she had missed out because of her weight. She started throwing up after almost every meal. By the time Jill developed her eating problem, she lived most of the time at college. In the summers she stayed in the college town and worked as a lifeguard. Jill's mother suspected something unusual was going on with her daughter.

When Jill came home once in a while on weekends, her mother followed her around after dinner. She reminded her daughter "about Karen Carpenter." Jill hated to hurt anyone's feelings. Unwilling to turn down her mother's lavish dinners, Jill ate them, then purged. Finally she decided to stop coming home.

Changes in the Wind?

In its May 15, 1990, cover story, "Getting Slim," *U.S. News & World Report* called dieting "America's obsession." The magazine reported a growing awareness that drastic dieting often does more harm than good. We now realize that too many dietary constraints can cause a person to have an even stronger craving for forbidden foods.

Are our habits really changing? A newspaper headline says, "It's No Longer In to Be Thin." *First for Women* magazine recently featured "The Look of the '90s." What is that look? "A toned healthy body is the goal," says Risa Sheppard, Los Angeles fitness specialist. "Thinness is not fitness. It's more important to be healthy and flexible."

Other hopeful signs crop up. In a recent interview a *Cosmopolitan* magazine cover girl described herself as six feet tall. Asked about her weight, she replied without concern, "I don't know how much I weigh."

Seventeen magazine introduced a feature, "School Zone," featuring *real* students from *real* high schools: "What we're looking for isn't waif-thin bodies or perfect noses. It's diversity. Individualism. Self-expression." And yet a spring issue of the magazine's classified section reveals that six of eight camp advertisements were for weight-loss camps.

Coping with the Media

How can you cope with the media's "Be slim!" message? The best way to fight back is to understand how and why you're being manipulated. Remember that the diet/fitness industry is big business and it wants *your* business.

Do yourself a favor. Analyze some of the ads you see in the magazine and TV commercials. Check for hidden messages. Remember that the skinny woman's figure you see on the television screen is the exact opposite of what has actually happened to women's bodies in the past twenty-five years. The average woman has become quite a few pounds *heavier.*

Some of the eating disorder organizations listed in Chapter 12 have intervened with large corporations to urge them to stop using advertising equating thinness with success or wealth. The National Association of Anorexia Nervosa and Associated Disorders (ANAD) persuaded the Hershey Corporation to discontinue the slogan, "You can never be too rich or too thin." The corporation responded to the pain of those who suffer from eating disorders. As one mother put it, "You *can* be too thin—it's called anorexia nervosa. And it kills."

More than a quarter of a century ago author Marshall McLuhan looked into the future in his book *The Medium Is the Massage.* He predicted that not only young children but many of the rest of us are beginning to believe whatever we see and hear from the media.

Do you?

CHAPTER 3

Ladies First? Women in Today's Society

A great revolution in American eating habits took place between 1880 and 1930, says historian Harvey Levenstein, author of *Revolution at the Table: The Transformation of the American Diet*. Until the late nineteenth century, doctors wrote books such as *How to be Plump*. A famous actress considered the epitome of beauty was Lillian Russell, who weighed in at two hundred pounds. Her rounded bosom and wide hips were the envy of women.

People of that time considered plumpness a sign of health. But over the years many forces in society have combined to persuade Americans that thinness is a sign of health and beauty.

Especially hard hit by the thinness revolution were women. David Garner and his team of researchers were among the first to point out the shift to a thinner ideal shape for females in America:

- Miss America contestants between 1959 and 1978 were thinner than in earlier years, and the winners were even thinner than the average contestants.
- The idealized woman, as illustrated in the center-fold of *Playboy* magazine, had become much thinner during the preceding twenty years.
- The number of diet articles in women's magazines increased by 20 percent between 1969 and 1978 over the preceding ten-year period.

Additional studies have found little change in attitudes. At a recent meeting of the American Psychological Association, Dr. Debbie Then reported on surveys done in 1992, which showed that two thirds of women who looked at models in women's magazines felt worse about themselves afterward.

Beauty for Whom?

Over the centuries many women have suffered to please men. In the nineteenth century American women endured tight corsets that squeezed their flesh. Ropes binding the toes of Japanese women prevented their feet from growing. Until the mid-twentieth century, most women didn't question their role. They were the quiet ones who did the housework, raised the children, and kept their men happy. Nowadays women are expected to do all the above plus work outside the home. No wonder some get confused and try to hide their confusion behind food issues. And, even though more women have moved into the workplace, ours is still a male-dominated society.

Carolyn: Male-Dominated

Carolyn developed her eating disorder relatively late in life. Although the incidents happened seven years ago, she remembers the circumstances well. Carolyn was a physical education teacher at a prep school, where she was also assistant athletic director. She coached a highly successful girls' volleyball team.

When the athletic director quit, Carolyn hoped to get his job. (The headmaster had promised to "hire from within.") Unfortunately for Carolyn, the rival school's volleyball coach, a friend of the headmaster, also wanted the job. He got it. The headmaster gave no reason for changing his mind and told Carolyn to "cooperate."

At about the same time, after ten childless years of marriage, Carolyn had a miscarriage. She thought the new athletic director expected her to become pregnant again right away. Then he would move in and take over her coaching job.

The new guy was a volleyball fanatic. He came un-invited to Carolyn's practices and taught new volleyball techniques to her students. After Carolyn had endured a year and a half of job-related stress, her teaching contract was not renewed.

In addition, Carolyn's husband lost his job because of standing up for something he believed in. Carolyn admired her husband for being true to his principles, but when he lost his job, she suffered too. Their combined income dropped from forty thousand dollars a year to fourteen thousand. Then she lost *her* job. They had one car repossessed and almost had to give up their house.

Throughout the preceding year Carolyn had been working out three times a week at a fitness center with one of the girls from the volleyball team. She also played adult volleyball for three hours every Monday night. One Monday after she had run two miles, worked out, and played volleyball, Carolyn got on the scale. She had lost three pounds in one day. If she did the same thing another day, she wondered, would she lose three more pounds? Carolyn considers that day the beginning of her long battle with anorexia and bulimia.

Carolyn calls herself "big-boned." She's five feet six and used to weigh 134 pounds. During her anorexic phase, Carolyn weighed herself four or five times a day. She kept telling herself she didn't "deserve" to eat. Or she would make herself accomplish "X" task first. If she did eat, she felt tortured with guilt. Why did you eat that? she'd ask herself. What good did it do to go running today?

The longest Carolyn ever went without food was three days. She chewed a lot of gum, ate hard candies, and drank black coffee. She considered those "foods" okay. No calories.

Finally Carolyn melted down to less than a hundred pounds. She kept telling herself that soon her menstrual periods would stop. Then she would take her behavior seriously and quit it.

When Carolyn began to grow facial hair, as sometimes happens in anorexia, she really got scared. Carolyn was a blonde, but the hair that grew on her face was brown. Her husband, who had tried to stay out of his wife's battles with food, had to say he didn't like her mustache. Carolyn herself didn't especially care for the dark hair that grew on her cheeks like a beard. She was beginning to look like Abraham Lincoln. With the help of a therapist, Carolyn finally was able to understand her worth as a person, and her battles with food stopped.

Is Fat a Feminist Issue?

In *Fat Is a Feminist Issue*, Susie Orbach writes that to understand eating disorders we must first look at the many meanings food has in the lives of women. To "go on a diet" without looking at those many meanings is a mistake. Even in these times when men often help with cooking and grocery shopping, women have the main responsibility for feeding the family.

Although society values the male role of breadwinner, the picture for women is not so clear. A "homemaker," a woman who cares for her family, is not always highly valued. However, if the woman chooses to work outside the home instead of becoming a wife and mother, many people feel sorry for her. They think she's missing something. Career women face special challenges. If they decide to have a career *in addition* to being a wife and mother, they risk neglecting their family, at least in society's view. Therefore, women must make difficult choices.

To fit the ideal of our culture, a woman must be thin. She must also prepare the food, but if she eats heartily and gets fat, she is considered a glutton. No wonder many females grow up confused about eating.

Some women, as well as men, are afraid to express their emotions directly. But women are more likely than men to nurture others by cooking for them.

Marilyn and Her Mom: Cooking and Eating for Love

Marilyn is fifty years old, weighs 195 pounds, and is a compulsive overeater. She doesn't remember a time when she didn't weigh close to two hundred. Pictures of her as a child, however, show her as normal sized.

Marilyn doesn't remember receiving many hugs from her parents. They rarely said, "I love you." And yet, Marilyn says, "I knew I was loved. Mom showed her love through baking—cookies, pies, cakes. She did the baking, and I did the eating. I swallowed up her love."

Don't Be Angry with Me!

No one likes an angry woman—screaming, crying, throwing dishes. Who needs it? In the past, women didn't feel comfortable expressing anger. If they did express it, they felt guilty and embarrassed afterward. Women's upbringing taught them to repress or hide their anger. They were programmed to be peacemakers and people-pleasers.

At the same time women are learning to be quiet, men learn that it's okay to get angry; it's important to be assertive. But for women, depression has been more acceptable. Depression is actually anger turned inward. Depression is often part of an eating disorder. Sometimes it's hard to tell whether depression has caused the eating disorder or the eating disorder has caused depression.

The situation may be changing, however. A recent newspaper headline commanded: "Get Mad and Get Glad: Message for Success to the Modern Woman." The article details a woman's response to a man's unfair treatment and tells how women can make anger work for them.

A waitress had been working since mid-afternoon. Her coworker, a waiter, had started work at 6:30 p.m. By midnight Annabel, the waitress, was exhausted and hoped to be sent home. The male manager, a friend of the waiter, sent him home instead. Annabel worked until 4 a.m.

Instead of crying and throwing things, Annabel decided

to control her anger. First she carefully planned her response; then she confronted the manager in a calm manner. She kept her anger on track to accomplish its purpose, which was to make the manager see her point of view. Because of Annabel's constructive anger, her relationship with the manager greatly improved. Thereafter he considered her needs and took her wishes seriously. The anecdote illustrates how a modern woman can use anger constructively. Annabel did not go home that day to binge and purge.

As hard as it is for women to use constructive anger with men, it is often even harder for them to show angry feelings to other women. But healthy anger shows that you take the other person seriously. Women are learning that anger expressed in the right way can have positive results.

Women as well as men often eat instead of expressing their feelings constructively. Rather than getting their anger out into the open, they literally stuff the feelings back down their throat with a big glob of food.

Harriet: A Feelings Swallower

Harriet's father deserted her and her mother when Harriet was only two years old. Even worse, he left them stuck in a small Texas town that Harriet's mother hated. Harriet spent most of her high school days trying to anticipate her mother's changing moods. Pushing down her own feelings in deference to her mother's, Harriet turned to food as her only joy. Finally, after Harriet had graduated from high school, her mother had saved enough money to move. By that time, however, Harriet had developed an eating disorder. She had spent a large part of her life trying to please her mother at the expense of her own body and happiness.

Many women are people-pleasers, and Harriet was no exception. Our culture is partly to blame for this unhappy state of affairs. Ever since time began, the "ideal" female has been quiet, sweet, and nurturing, the kind of person who looks after others while denying her own needs and wants.

Like My Body? Are You Kidding?

For more than twenty years, researchers have studied girls' and boys' attitudes toward their bodies. Almost 100 percent of those studies show girls wanting to be thinner and boys wanting to be heavier. A study of a thousand high school students showed half of the girls wanting smaller hips, thighs, or waists. While the boys worried about being underweight, 70 percent of the girls wanted to lose weight. Yet only one fourth of the girls were actually overweight.

Ruth: The Bridesmaid Became Anorexic

Ruth is a forty-year-old mother of three girls. Never, she says, will she say anything negative to her daughters about weight or food. She made that resolution after two memorable incidents—one when she was fourteen and the other when she was eighteen.

At age fourteen, Ruth and her cousin Shirley were invited to be junior bridesmaids in the wedding of a second cousin. Shirley's mother (Aunt Bea), who worked in a fancy dress shop, ordered the junior bridesmaids' outfits. She ordered a size eight for Ruth. Shirley, who was taller and chubbier for her age, got a size ten. Ruth remembers the humiliating moment when the dresses arrived. Not only was Shirley's dress too big, but Ruth's was too tight. To fit into the "ugly, absurd dress," Ruth went on a crash diet and lost seventeen pounds before the wedding. Her moment of triumph came when she walked down the aisle in the size eight dress. Nevertheless, Ruth recalls, she felt miserable in her braces and in the flowery headdress that fell across her forehead.

At some point during the next four years, Ruth's family moved away, and she regained the lost weight. On a visit to Ruth's home, Aunt Bea took one look at her and remarked, "I see we're getting fatty again." Horrified, Ruth went on a second crash diet. This time her forty-pound weight loss put her in the anorexic category.

While boys are expressing their competitive natures through sports and games, girls are often competing through weight and physical appearance. Studies of preschoolers have shown that even at that early age being pretty is considered important. Girls as young as five are already worried about gaining weight.

And things don't improve with the years. In some schools 80 percent of fourth-grade girls are already "dieting." Even more significant, boys of the same age said that fourth-grade girls should be able to control themselves and not get fat. Another author studied sixth-grade girls. Those who considered themselves not popular thought of themselves as neither pretty enough nor skinny enough.

In a recent newspaper column, Stephanie Brush of Tribune Media Services writes, "The entire history of the twentieth century can be traced back to the fact that every fifteen-year-old girl on earth hates her ankles." Ms. Brush is kidding, of course, but there is much truth in what she says. Recalling her own teen years, Ms. Brush says that she and her friends used to draw pictures of themselves. Her self-portrait had the word "Hindenburg" (a blimp) drawn next to each thigh. She drew tiny hams where her knees should have been and pig hooves for her feet. This is only one example of girls hating their normal body curves.

Men's fitness goals are usually different from women's. Men want to be fit for health. For example, they don't want to have a heart attack. Women and girls are more likely to exercise in pursuit of thinness. A *Glamour* magazine survey showed that 95 percent of thirty-three thousand females had used exercise for weight control.

Coping with Society

To cope with society's expectations we have to understand that often what seems "real" is not. Television and movies are not real. Thinking that "thin is better" is not real either. Women must not let themselves be devalued by equating their self-worth with shape and size. Thinking realistically may help, but a person may also need the assistance of a therapist or a support group to counter the unrealistic messages of the culture.

We can learn to recognize diets for what they are, dangerous and unhealthy. Doctors and others who work with people who have eating disorders sometimes teach them to use "coping phrases," such as: "I will eat my dinner, and it will not make me fat," or "I need to eat to be healthy," or "In spite of my beliefs about society's expectations, I am already quite thin."

Speak Up!

Being assertive does not mean being aggressive or physically pushy. Assertiveness means standing up for your needs and getting them met in healthy ways without hurting others. Everyone needs to feel safe, to have friends and satisfying relationships, to be listened to and to be noticed, to have some control over her life, to have time for fun, and to have time for herself. A person who is totally unassertive may let others "walk all over her." She may believe she is unworthy of a happy life.

Low self-esteem is definitely part of the eating disorder picture. A person with low self-worth may turn to food or control over food for comfort. Instead, people can learn to value themselves and find healthy ways of self-nurturing. Assertiveness training may be helpful. Community centers and schools offer classes in which you can learn to speak up. Also you can find books on the subject in your local library.

CHAPTER 4

Families

Ask any expert on child-rearing where kids grow best. The answer is certain to be: "In families, of course." That is why adoption workers spend their time finding families for "waiting children," children in need of families. But at the same time we sing the praises of families, we tend to blame them when something goes wrong with *one* of their members. Parents often take it on the chin for being too much involved in their children's lives or not involved enough. Families in today's society are pressured to do everything right but seldom have the kind of helping network (grandparents, aunts, uncles, cousins) that families had in the past. We also know that families are only *one* of the many influences on children in today's society.

IT MIGHT BE IN YOUR GENES

Experts used to blame families for causing eating disorders, but recent studies raise the question of a possible genetic link. Girls with anorexic siblings are ten to twenty times more likely than others to develop an eating disorder themselves. Those with family histories of alcoholism and/or depression are also at risk.

Mothers/Daughters

Mothers are role models for girls, but what happens when Mom has trouble with her role in society or with her own identity? Boys and girls have the same goal in growing up: to separate from their parents and establish their own identities. Because Mother is the main caregiver, her children have a harder time separating from her than they do from their father. Boys have an easier task; they have always been different from their mother. A girl may feel very much *like* her mother and take on many of her mother's feelings.

When a daughter becomes an adolescent, she may have a tense and conflicted relationship with her mother. Both may feel frustrated with their roles in society and not even realize their frustration. Mothers and daughters may be ambivalent. Mothers *want* their daughter to be like them and *don't want* their daughter to be like them. Daughters *want* to leave their mother and *don't want* to leave her. Some girls are afraid of growing up and being like their mother. They are confused by the mothers they see on TV—thin, well dressed, with a handsome husband, a clean house, a high-paying job, well-behaved children, and a perpetual smile. Is it any wonder the daughter asks herself: How come my mom's not like that?

These mother-daughter conflicts and subtle messages become mixed up with eating and food. A daughter's fatness may be saying to her mother: "I'm well padded; I can go out into the world and not get hurt." Or a daughter who is too far from the norm (either too skinny or very chubby) may subconsciously use her weight to say to her mother: "I can't take care of myself very well, Mom. I still need your help."

One way a daughter can try to show independence from her mother and express her own identity is to make sure that her weight is the *opposite* of her mother's. Try this exercise in observation. Check out your friends and their mothers. Do you find that chubby mothers tend to have skinny daughters and thin mothers often have heavier daughters?

The Female Connection

We are finally beginning to realize one important characteristic of women: Most do not *want* to separate. Women's strength comes from their connections—to their families and to their friends.

Stacey and Candy Standridge: Sisters in Distress

When Stacey was a sophomore transfer student at the University of Nebraska, she went to the health service because of her problems with food. She had spent her freshman year at a small, private liberal arts college in the state of Washington, where she was an anorexic member of the cross-country team.

Originally her parents had encouraged Stacey to go away to school. Her preoccupation with food and her unhappiness with everyone and everything were driving them crazy. After winter break Stacey's sister Candy had to practically *push* her sister onto the airplane for the trip back to college. Her mother told Stacey she had to spend at least one year at Raintree College so they could "get their money's worth."

The Standridge family valued slimness. In her freshman year at Raintree, Stacey finally seemed to get the family message, as well as society's message. She existed on the berries she found along the road on her long daily runs. Although she had lost thirty-eight pounds, Stacey never came to the attention of the health service at Raintree. By the next year she had talked her parents into letting her transfer to the university about two hours from home.

When Stacey told her story at the health service, the counselor mentioned (among other things) that because of family dynamics, her sister Candy was "at risk" for the development of an eating disorder.

Why? Because members of the girls' family did not express feelings; they stressed appearances instead. Mrs. Standridge was a skinny, modish, fifty-year-old golf player who got her "kicks" at the country club. Mr. Standridge, a successful stockbroker, got his kicks from his job. It seemed to his daughters that work was more important to him than his family.

Over the years as Stacey's eating disorder careened out of control, Candy vowed never to go through the hell of her sister's experience. And yet, as Stacey's counselor had predicted, when Candy got to college she had her own eating problems. Here's what she wrote in her diary:

"My face looks so fat! But Wendy has a fat face, and she has a boyfriend. I don't know why I equate fat with failure and skinny with success.

"Fat = Failure?
"Skinny = Success?

"Why am I so obsessed with my weight? Maybe it's because I *am* fat: five feet, two inches and 129 pounds. Well, I'm going to stop worrying about it. I really am. I'm going to start my new cheerful outlook—tomorrow."

*   *   *

Sometimes father-daughter relationships are worth scrutinizing. Let's hear what Claire has to say. "My father is very prejudiced against fat people and always stresses appearances. He's never happy unless I'm underweight. If I gain a few pounds I can feel his dissatisfaction. That makes it hard for me to feel good about myself." A daughter who has been conditioned to strive for male attention may do anything, including losing excessive amounts of weight, to gain her father's approval.

In addition, children may come from a family in which they have been overfed or underfed. Sasha's mother made sure she never had junk food of any kind in the house, and she watched like a hawk every morsel that passed her daughter's lips. When Sasha went to her friends' houses she "pigged out" on any kind of junk food she could get her hands on. Much later, when Sasha was old enough to have her own apartment, she made sure she had enough junk food on hand at all times, especially for bingeing on at night.

Another problem for some families is that rules that worked well when the children were young may be too restrictive for teenagers. Most teens want more privileges as they grow older and more freedom to run their own lives. Sometimes parents have a hard time letting go of the reins, becoming too involved in their children's lives. A control problem develops, and it may reveal itself around food.

Young people with eating disorders have usually picked up the family message that they must achieve great things. Only by reaching a pinnacle of near perfection will they feel they can be worthy of the family honor. In such cases the family sends subtle messages as to whether or not the child has "made it." Rarely can the child be "good enough." That leads to feelings of failure, incompetence, inadequacy, anger, and finally (possibly) an eating disorder.

Brad: Thou Shalt Not!

Brad's religious upbringing was filled with "Thou shalt nots." His parents instilled in him a desire to succeed but failed to give him the feeling that he was okay just as himself. When Brad did his best but failed to attain perfection, he berated himself. It was not surprising that at age thirteen he began to consider his body less than perfect. His father's comment after the last soccer game of the season didn't help much. "Good game," said Dad. "It's too bad you can't run as fast as you used to. Too much weight to carry around."

At that point Brad instituted his rigid diet. He lived on one carefully measured cup of cereal with skim milk per day. He started to do five hundred jumping jacks every morning. Alarmed at Brad's self-inflicted punishment, his mother took him to the pediatrician.

"Hey, man," said the doctor, "why are you trying to hurt yourself?" As the result of his doctor's words, Brad gave up most of his exercise and all of his diet. Ultimately, Brad became a high-achieving family therapist. Not only did he want to try to understand his own family-of-origin, but he wanted to help other people understand theirs.

Finally, family members often pass down these problems from one generation to the next—unless they get help. John Bradshaw writes and lectures about families. Parents commit what he calls "soul murder" every day, he says. Most often, they don't realize that they're doing anything wrong. They are merely using the way they were raised as their model of parenting. In their efforts to bring up their children to conform to society's expectations, they deny the children expression of feelings, especially angry feelings and sexual feelings. When a person loses contact with her feelings, she loses contact with her body. Once people get a clue to what went wrong in their family, they are in a better position to do something about it.

The Burris Family: A Generational Saga

Mom (Janet Burris) was an only child. When she was seven her father died, and her mother had to go back to work full time. Janet spent a lot of time with her grandmother, who lived next door. Neither Mom nor Grandma drove a car; all of them went everywhere on the bus.

Janet could hardly wait to marry and have children of her own. She thought of her future children as lumps of clay she would mold. She would sculpt them into the kind of person she wished she could have been. Her children would be her second chance at life.

When Janet met the man of her dreams, she moved a thousand miles away from her mother and grandmother. Although she hated to leave, a strong thought lurked in the back of her mind: She would be able to raise her children in her own way with little interference from Mom and Grandma.

She had fantasies of the things they would do, things she never had a chance to try—piano lessons, dance lessons, swim team, soccer, softball. Janet imagined how she would meet her children's every need so that they could have the happy childhood she had missed.

Janet's husband Greg was happy to leave most of the child-rearing to his wife. He was somewhat remote—like his father before him. After dinner he hid behind the newspaper. He considered raising children women's work.

The first two children were boys. Janet did her best with them, but she didn't really understand boys. She had not had a brother to grow up with, and her father had died when she was young.

When their third child arrived, Janet vowed that in raising Emily she would try hard to do everything "right." Emily went everywhere with Janet, and she had even more lessons than her brothers. Janet derived tremendous satisfaction from the things her daughter did well. But when Emily experienced failures, such as forgetting her entire piece in the piano recital, Janet felt crushed. Janet needed her daughter to boost her own shaky self-esteem. Furthermore, she had trouble accepting the fact that everyone makes mistakes, that mistake-making is the way we learn.

When Emily became a teenager, she felt suffocated by her mother's excessive concern. Janet showed her love with worry. Janet had not gotten many hugs in her family and wasn't used to showing affection. The worry message came across in a different way to Emily. If my mother worries so much about me, Emily thought, she must think I'm not very competent. Worry also built a wall between them and kept them from achieving real closeness.

Janet didn't know how to give Emily the message that she loved her for herself, for the wonderful, unique person her daughter was. Emily always felt that she had to prove her worth in some way, that she had to earn her right to be alive, to be loved.

In addition, Janet was always there, "in my face," as Emily put it. If Emily came home a few minutes after her 11 p.m. curfew her mother freaked out; she panicked.

Actually, Janet wouldn't allow Emily to go out at all unless she had practiced both her instruments, piano and saxophone. A no-practice day did not fit with Mom's version of Emily's future. Both parents wanted Emily to get a scholarship to college.

For as long as Emily could remember, the first thing Grandma said when she came for a visit was, "Hasn't she put on some weight?" On leaving for home this time, Grandma took Emily aside and promised her a new dress "when she lost a few pounds."

The week after Grandma left, Janet began suggesting that Emily accompany her on the long walks she took every day. The pressure to lose weight and the overcontrol that came from three generations was too much for Emily. At age seventeen she developed anorexia nervosa. Somehow she had to prove to her family that she could control one area of her life.

Emily's story illustrates how a family, even with the best intentions, can play a part in the development of an eating disorder. Also, we can see how one generation can pass to the next a tendency to an eating disorder. When did Emily's anorexia begin and how? No one in the family realized until much later, when the whole family participated in therapy, that Emily's eating disorder had begun generations ago.

The McCarthy Family: Unlikely Actors

Rachel describes her father, an attorney, as an alcoholic and her mother, a veterinarian, as a workaholic. Rachel became the person with the eating disorder. No one confronted her parents about their "holisms." These kinds of problems are more common in families of people with eating disorders than in the general population.

Rachel says she was aware of her eating disorder from the moment it began. "After spending the summer in Europe at age sixteen, I had gained twenty-five pounds. I wanted to be thin, and I had heard of a girl who threw up every day after eating dinner. Because of her eating disorder, this girl got a lot of attention. I thought that if I were to do the same I would lose weight and get attention. At nineteen, after three years of misery, I admitted that I had lost control. I asked for help. Although I knew I had an eating disorder (bingeing, purging, abusing laxatives), I didn't understand the reasons at first. Eventually I learned that I was having problems emotionally—coping with life and the stresses of college."

During the McCarthy girls' teenage years, Kim, the older sister, had been the pleaser/do-gooder. Rachel was the rebel. When members of the family fought, Kim tried to patch things up. She went to college with the idea of majoring in fine arts, but her parents said no. Fine arts, they said, had no practical application. Kim got her degree in psychology. Then she went to graduate school hoping to study dance, but again her parents didn't approve. Finally she applied to law school. That pleased her parents.

Kim has always been thin; she watches her weight carefully. Most people would call her beautiful. No matter what she studies, Kim gets As. She is the family "Heroine."

Rachel, a bit on the chunky side, is still struggling to "find herself." As she wrestles with bulimia, she works at low-paying restaurant jobs and barely supports herself. She uses most of her income for food, which she eats and then throws up. And although Rachel hasn't admitted it even to herself, she has developed a problem with alcohol. Rachel is the family "Scapegoat."

The McCarthy family illustrates what often happens in a dysfunctional family no matter what the cause of the dysfunction. Like Kim and Rachel, family members get locked into rigid roles. To maintain a sense of stability in their wacky family system, they accept their roles. No one is being honest; therefore, no one can be truly free.

Most often the spouse of an alcoholic takes on the role of the "major enabler." Others in the family may be "minor enablers." They cover up for the person with the problem, allowing the family to protect that person and to maintain the status quo. To outsiders the group appears normal. But keeping the secret (or secrets) is hard on family members, and finally something cracks under the strain.

Because of her position as oldest child (rather than because of her personality or other factors), Kim played the role of Heroine in her family. The Hero/Heroine is noteworthy because of what he or she accomplishes. This person achieves something that the world notices and values and thus gives the family a sense of self-worth.

When the second child comes along, the Hero role is already taken. As a subconscious way of getting some of the parents' attention, the second child often becomes the Scapegoat, taking the blame for others. Negative attention is better than no attention at all. Rachel became the focus of her family's concern and the McCarthy family Scapegoat.

Other roles, such as Lost Child or Mascot, can be found in larger families. In smaller families one child may take several roles.

The person with an eating disorder may be a Lost Child. While growing up, the Lost Child doesn't attempt to force himself or herself into center stage in the manner of the Scapegoat. He simply retreats to the wings, where he goes about life unnoticed. This person feels unimportant and perhaps neglected. He may retreat into a fantasy world, spending time in his room daydreaming. His few pleasures may include reading, watching television, listening to music—and eating or abusing substances. Because he has never really learned to cope with the outside world, he becomes even more isolated as he gets older. The Lost Child suffers from low self-esteem as a result of being ignored. Because no one has ever expected much of him, he may expect little of himself. The Lost Child may overeat or use drugs to try to erase feelings of emptiness and loneliness.

Jake: A Lost Child

Jake, the third child in his family, is still living at home at age twenty-seven. His older brother Sam, thirty-one, is the family Hero. Sam is a high-achieving astrophysicist with poor people skills. Sister Phyllis, twenty-nine, is in jail for stealing jewelry, selling drugs, and driving under the influence.

Jake was an "accident"; his parents had planned to stop at two children. Shortly after his birth his parents divorced, and his mother had to go back to work. She had few job skills but finally found a job in a day-care center. Jake's development was slow; he walked late, talked late, and had learning disabilities. He learned rather quickly, however, that in his family it was better to be "seen and not heard." In elementary school Jake kept to himself; food was his only friend. As he moved into high school, he ignored his mother's urgings to "get some exercise" or to stop eating doughnuts and soda pop for breakfast. After all, Jake thought, if people in his family cared so little about him, why should he care for himself?

Jake made it through his freshman year of college but flunked out as a sophomore. By that time he recognized himself as a compulsive eater. He joined a support group, which gave him the emotional strength to confront the fact that he had never had a relationship with a girl in spite of daydreaming about women much of the time.

On the other hand, the person with an eating disorder could be the family Mascot. Often this person is the youngest child. By his or her antics, the Mascot diverts the family members' attention from their pain. That is her family role. She may be a clown or be hyperactive, using whatever means she can to capture a bit of attention for herself. She presents a smiling face to the world, but inside she feels empty and lonely. She may use alcohol or drugs to numb her pain, or she may use food.

People play roles when they are trying to adapt to an unhealthy situation. Of course, all of us play roles at times, but when playing a role becomes a person's lifelong way of operating, it is time to seek help.

Brothers/Sisters

Earlier we discussed parent-child conflicts in families, but one researcher has pointed out a possible connection between eating disorders and siblings. Karen Lewis describes five kinds of messages siblings may try to give to brothers and sisters through their eating disorder:

1. The *connecting message* says, "I'll bring us together." In a family in which siblings have little to do with each other, bulimia or anorexia in one member may give the rest something to talk about.
2. The *equalizing message* says, "I have a problem too. We're not so different." The "good" child in the family may use this message as a way of proving to her brothers and sisters that she is no better than they are.
3. The *deflecting message* can be a way of turning the family's attention from another member's more serious problem. Lacy Arthur, age seventeen, a high school student with outstanding grades, had bulimia. Her sister Beverly, twenty, had problems with overuse of alcohol. Lacy still lived at home, but her parents were paying for Beverly's apartment and hardly noticed her. By getting the parents to focus on her eating disorder, Lacy helped her sister by deflecting attention away from Beverly.
4. The *peacemaking message* is one way of bringing the family together in some kind of harmony. By concentrating on the eating problem and what to do about it, they have a common goal.
5. The *dirty-fighting message* may be used by a sibling who feels she has had less attention in the family than the others. She may use her eating disorder as a way of getting more attention and thereby getting back at her siblings.

The Tappen Family: Sibling Rivalry

On the surface the Tappen family appeared to be normal, with no more than the usual family problems. When

Estelle went away to college, however, she developed a severe eating disorder. During winter break her strange behaviors riled the entire family. At night while everyone else slept in their beds with visions of sugarplums dancing in their heads, Estelle roamed the house, zeroing in on the kitchen.

Her brothers began to call her "the Midnight Stalker," a nickname Estelle did not appreciate. Her younger sister Brittany, age twelve, barely noticed. She was too busy practicing for her ballet debut in "The Nutcracker" with the city's symphony orchestra. Mrs. Tappen was exhausted from working all day and then driving Brittany back and forth to rehearsals. Mom had little tolerance for Estelle's kitchen antics.

Later, in family therapy sessions, Estelle was able to admit that she had always been jealous of Brittany, the youngest child. Estelle considered her little sister cuter, more talented, and favored by their parents.

Estelle's eating disorder may have been an unconscious effort to steal back some parental attention. When those motivations came out in the open, Estelle gained a better understanding of her problem.

Coping with Your Family

Nick Stinnett and John DeFrain, both professors of family studies, have written a book called *Secrets of Strong Families.* Through research with three thousand families over a ten-year period, these experts identified six of the most prominent traits of healthy families: commitment, appreciation, communication, time, spiritual wellness, and coping ability.

Commitment: Having common goals, promoting the welfare of other family members, making family a priority—in these ways family members show their commitment to each other.

Appreciation: Too often parents and children waste a great deal of energy criticizing each other. Some family therapists give each family member the task of saying one nice thing every day to every other member of the family.

Communication: People in strong families spend a lot of time talking to each other—and listening to each other.

Time: Members of healthy families report spending both quality time and quantity time together. Many families report improved relationships after they have made time for a "family night" each week. Perhaps you could be the one to suggest dinner together once a week, followed by family games.

Spiritual Wellness: Strong families share a sense of a higher power or greater good in life, whether or not they attend formal religious services.

Coping Ability: Because no family can go through life free of conflict and stress, the ability to cope with whatever life brings is an important characteristic shared by those in healthy families.

Your family may be able to gather these strengths through reading and enrichment courses or by consulting a family counselor.

One of the most important things in coping with your family is to realize that all the members are doing the best they can given their particular circumstances. This understanding will give you the strength to do what you need to do to start the healing process. If you're lucky, you'll get the support of your family. You may find that when you begin to open up to family members about your fears and concerns, they may be more open with you. Through your eating disorder you may cause positive changes to occur in your family's ways of relating. If you do decide to go to a family therapist, be sure to find one acquainted with eating disorder issues. For example, certain family members may learn that they no longer need to play the role of the enabler. Family enablers are doing no one, including themselves, a favor. Girls may need assertiveness training, if only to make their needs known within the family. Above all, remember that the family is only *one* of the many influences on young people today.

Give your family a break!

CHAPTER ◇ 5

Feeling Your Feelings

O ne of the most valuable things to learn is that an eating disorder is not just a problem with weight or food. Developing an eating disorder is the way some people *use* food to try to deal with emotions and inner conflicts.

Virginia, a freshman at a large Midwestern university, had a problem with bulimia for many years. She wrote this in her emotions diary:

"I'm bummed out because I felt lost in the crowd tonight. There are so many beautiful girls here. I saw people I knew in high school—Nancy (skinny as ever and gorgeous as usual); Greta (who looks tiny, tan, and really fantastic, and who is on a diet to lose ten *more* pounds); and Rosie (who looks like a totally different person—skinny, mainly). I'm bummed because I feel inadequate and fat (because of all the skinny, beautiful girls). I feel so insecure here. I have to get out of this feeling. I have to stop caring what other people think of me. I want to be happy and stop worrying that I'm not exercising enough, studying enough, partying enough, or keeping busy enough. I'm sick of being so discontented."

Everyone experiences loneliness or emptiness at times, but some people feel that way most of the time. They try to extinguish their uncomfortable feelings by eating excessively or not eating at all. The inability to express feelings in a healthy way is probably at the core of most eating disorders. In *The Deadly Diet*, Terence Sandbek says that if a person with an eating disorder can learn to deal with destructive emotions, she will make great progress. He identifies six of those emotions.

The first is **depression**, an unhealthy emotion that makes a person feel like a wet dishrag. Depression is different from sadness. Sadness is a normal emotion that people experience, for example, when someone they love dies. No one can say how long grief should last. In one famous survey, people were asked how long they thought a person should grieve after the death of someone close. Most of those questioned said about a month. Although there is no right answer, the truth is closer to a year or even two years in some cases. Some people point out that we experience little deaths and losses each day. It is normal to be sad about these smaller losses, such as a friend's moving away. But after we grieve for a while, maybe cry a bit, or talk to someone, we're okay again. Grief and sadness can help us heal and become stronger people. On the other hand, depression destroys.

Virginia's feelings at the beginning of this chapter are a good example of destructive emotions. Virginia felt unworthy and depressed. No matter what she did, she didn't feel that she could measure up to those around her. Depression may lead to eating disorder, eating disorder leads to depression, and the cycle continues.

Guilt is an emotion that can be either constructive or destructive, depending on how we use it. When we use guilt as a spur to our conscience to improve relationships with others, it is constructive. But when we play the same guilt-trip "tapes" over and over in our brain, guilt can be destructive. People who are overwhelmed with guilt pepper their self-talk with words such as "should," "have to," "must," and "ought." They don't need punishment from anyone else; they punish themselves. Guilt pops up all the time in the journals kept by people with eating disorders: "I binged last night; today I feel so guilty." This is the same emotion that can trigger the next binge, which makes the person feel even more guilty.

People with healthy self-esteem don't wallow in guilt. Still, no one is perfect. We all do hurtful things at times. If we *have* hurt someone, we can do our best to apologize or make amends. That is one of the twelve steps in such programs as Alcoholics Anonymous (AA) and Overeaters Anonymous (OA).

Another related but even more deeply ingrained and troublesome feeling is shame. Whereas guilt comes from *doing* something harmful to ourselves or to others, shame comes from feeling that we *are* bad. Shame exists at the very central part of our being.

Christy Henrich, former Olympic-class gymnast, died of complications of anorexia and bulimia. On July 26, 1994, one newspaper reporter said that shame and guilt fueled her eating disorder. Earlier Henrich herself had said, "It feels like there's a beast inside of me, like a monster!"

Most people carry shame around with them like an invisible backpack. "Shame on you!" a parent might have said to try to change your behavior for the better. Or your mother and father may have "shamed" *you* because of the shame *they* feel. If discontented with their own lot in life, parents feel pain. When the pain gets too intense, they start putting the "shoulds" and "oughts" onto their children's shoulders. In that way children pick up shame messages. Bradshaw calls the transfer of shame "passing the hot potato."

Dr. Charles Whitfield tells us that we have to acknowledge our shame and work through it in order to become real human beings. He calls this unexpressed part of ourself our "child within." This inner child (or real self) longs to get out and express itself. But because we were silenced in our families when we tried to express our emotions, our child within is afraid to speak out.

Negative compulsive behaviors result. Some people abuse alcohol, some use nicotine or other drugs, some become addicted to destructive relationships. Whitfield says, "It may involve overeating, overworking, overspending, or even overattending self-help group meetings."

Some people may never be able to figure out where their feelings of shame came from. Sadie, a compulsive eater, remembers quitting her tap dancing class at age five because she feared "messing up" in the dance recital. Roslyn, a bulimic, revealed in a support group that she would rather be arrested for jaywalking than press the "walk" button and cross the street "with all those people looking at me."

Helplessness is a third useless emotion. Two alternatives are strength and weakness. No one can be strong all the time; it isn't normal. Everyone has periods of weakness. If we accept the fact that all human beings have weaknesses, we will be able to take the steps necessary to improve our lives. As they say in Overeaters Anonymous, "We come together not from strength but from weakness." That tells us that someone with an eating disorder cannot cure herself but needs help.

Fourth on the list of destructive emotions is **resentment**. When this emotion takes over, the person harboring it is eaten alive by it. Self-destructive behaviors result. On the flip side of resentment are tolerance, love, and understanding. A person with an eating disorder who hates her parents for whatever damage they seem to have done to her, or for the mistakes they made in raising her, is not likely to go very far in recovery. It will be more helpful if she is able to gain some understanding of her parents' life circumstances during her childhood.

On the journey to understanding we may feel anger. Anger is an emotion that can be useful in changing an unacceptable situation. Experts now believe that well-used, controlled anger is a powerful tool that both men and women can use to change their jobs and personal relationships for the better.

Becky, a participant in a twelve-step program, put it this way: "I'm angry. I've followed the rules, I've worked the steps, and I'm still not cured. I'm angry." Those in the group understood. Some of them felt angry too. They accepted Becky's anger and were willing to listen and give her support for her feelings. By expressing her anger to sympathetic listeners, Becky moved a step closer to recovery.

Unhealthy anxiety is a fifth destructive emotion. Unhealthy anxiety and healthy anxiety are very different emotions. Everyone feels anxious in certain situations. The lead in the school play uses healthy anxiety to help give a good performance. A person running for a student council office uses healthy anxiety to put some "oomph" into a speech. On the other hand, unhealthy anxiety may prevent another person from auditioning for the play or even running for office.

Heather, a compulsive eater, described her anxiety

about being in her best friend's wedding. The wedding itself didn't unnerve Heather, but the buffet afterward did. "I've been doing so well," she said, "but I'm afraid I'll blow it at the reception. It's not a sit-down affair; it's the kind of party where everyone just roams around and eats." Heather used some healthy anxiety to make a plan. She would eat before the wedding and then, with the help of her built-in support system, not touch food at all during the party.

The pleasant side of anxiety is a sense of calm peacefulness. All of us, once in a while, experience this comfortable state of affairs. We wish we could feel calm all the time, but considering life's hectic pace, we have to live with some anxiety.

The last, sometimes paralyzing, unhealthy emotion is **fear**. Some compulsive overeaters who have insulated themselves with excess pounds fear getting thin. They're afraid that if they are thin people may want to get close to them. Others use excess weight to make people think they're incompetent. They don't want to have to achieve or try to reach expectations that they think are too high. For some people being fat feels safer. Those with anorexia or bulimia may fear gaining only a few pounds. They fear that even one or two extra pounds will make them less desirable. Or they worry that once they gain a pound they'll keep gaining weight and never be able to stop.

Those who feel alone and unsupported may fear living with all the problems life presents. Stephanie, a participant in an eating disorder support group, admitted that she had begun to get up at night to eat. This behavior scared her. Not only that, but life itself scared her. That is why one of the tools of recovery in Overeaters Anonymous is the telephone. Members learn to ask for help as well as giving help to others.

In *Feel the Fear and Do It Anyway*, Susan Jeffers explains how to keep fear from holding us back. Only by feeling the fear and doing whatever we need to do to reach our goals can we grow and achieve an authentic sense of well-being.

Whose Problem Is It?

Some people think we should look at eating disorders in the context of codependency. The word **codependent** originally described someone who, in a relationship with an alcoholic, denied her own feelings in order to survive. Nowadays the word is used in many different ways. Codependence can mean relying on someone or some substance outside yourself to meet your needs instead of relying on your own self-worth. Basically, a person who is codependent tries to get his or her needs met in unhealthy ways. A person with an eating disorder is using food in unhealthy ways. Therefore we may call a person with an eating disorder codependent.

The relatives of the person with an eating disorder may also be codependent. For example, a mother may devote several years of her life to trying to cure her daughter of bulimia. The mother begs her daughter to give up vomiting after every meal. Or good ol' Mom goes to the grocery store every day to replenish food consumed during her daughter's nightly binges.

According to Judy Hollis in *Fat Is a Family Affair*, "Recovery from an eating disorder requires a precious journey to find the real self." A person has to learn to nurture self with the support of others. That support cannot come from codependent relationships but from the kind of help that validates the person's struggle to become her own person. Food won't do it. As a result of this inner journey, the person's relationships will become more healthy. The journey may not be short or easy, but it is sure to be worthwhile.

The first step is for the person to admit that she has a problem with food and with the way she has tried to get help in the past. Second, she must try to find new and more healthy ways to get help from others.

We'll talk more about getting help later, but first let's try to understand what causes a person to look outside herself (and sometimes to do destructive things to herself) in an attempt to get her needs met.

Loretta: A Tough Cookie

Loretta was a pretty, dark-haired, dark-eyed girl, adopted at age six. Even at that tender age Loretta put on a tough exterior, something like a turtle's shell. The few friends she had were a bit afraid of her. If people offended her, Loretta did not hesitate to tell them off. For example, some of the kids at school insisted on calling her "Lori" even though she had told them hundreds of times that her name was Loretta. Sometimes she even scared her parents; they hesitated to confront her or to correct her when she did something naughty.

In her late twenties Loretta joined a support group for compulsive eaters. While in the group, Loretta remembered some interesting things about her younger self. On her twelfth birthday, Loretta said, she had requested a chocolate cake with chocolate frosting. She ate almost all of the cake herself. A year later on a trip to a dude ranch with her parents, she polished off eight jelly-filled doughnuts on a breakfast horseback ride. At home she had made a habit of consuming seven pieces of rye toast (slathered with orange marmalade) every day for breakfast.

Loretta also revealed some of the details of a backpacking trip she had taken with a small group from school. At age fifteen the first thing she packed for the trip was the security blanket she had somehow managed to hang onto since her babyhood days in her birthfamily. Loretta considered the blanket her only tie to her birthmother.

Around the campfire during a sharing time, Loretta had confided her feelings about the blanket. As she talked, a tear rolled down her check. "I usually don't discuss my feelings," she said, wiping at the tear with the back of her hand.

"Feelings?" said a classmate. "You? I never knew you had any."

Perhaps if Loretta could have dealt earlier with her feelings about her birthparents and her adoption, she would not have developed an eating disorder. After participating in the support group, Loretta decided to undertake a search for her birthmother. As a result, she not only discovered the answers to questions about her heredity, she also experienced a wonderful sense of freedom she had never felt before.

Many authorities believe that any parenting less than total nurturing can cause codependence. Using that definition, all of us (even those parented in the most well-meaning way) are products of abuse and could be called codependent. Parents with the best of motives may have unintentionally abused their children.

Because everyone is codependent to a certain extent, some experts dismiss the whole concept as meaningless. You can decide for yourself whether the idea makes sense to you. Let's see how it applies to the Horsely family.

Jeff and Cindy Horsely: Victims of Love

Jeff and Cindy were born into a loving family. Their parents were twenty-two and twenty-six when Jeff was born. Betty and Bob wanted children very much and tried to raise them well. The couple thought they should know enough about raising children. Bob was a social worker who dealt with abused children every working day. Betty was a nurse who worked with sick kids on a hospital pediatric unit.

When Jeff was born, Betty and Bob were thrilled. Betty quit work to devote full time to child-rearing. They loved Jeff so much that they were excited when Cindy came along eighteen months later.

Jeff was a shy little boy, but Betty and Bob got him into a Montessori preschool as soon as he was potty trained at two and a half years old. They wanted him to learn to play with other children, stand up for himself, and be assertive. Because the parents themselves were unassertive, it seemed even more important to them that their children develop the qualities they lacked.

When Jeff fell down and skinned his knees, Betty was afraid to cuddle him too much. She wanted her son to be brave, to be a "little man." As Jeff got older his parents signed him up for competitive sports so that he would experience the give-and-take of athletics. Bob attended most of Jeff's games and pointed out the things he did wrong. Bob's own father had never shown much affection (he considered hugs and kisses for women), but Bob had always known he was loved. Without realizing it, Bob raised his son the way he himself had been raised.

Cindy was a darling girl with blonde curls and blue eyes. Betty hoped her daughter would reflect her careful upbringing. She dressed Cindy like a little doll. Although she hated to sew, she made many of Cindy's clothes. She wanted her daughter to be "all girl," but she never told Cindy how cute she looked. She didn't want her to be conceited.

Betty had considered herself a fat child even though she wasn't. She carefully watched her own weight as well as her daughter's.

Betty also became deeply involved in her children's education. When Cindy got a strict teacher in fourth grade, Betty asserted herself, which was hard for her. She got the principal to move Cindy to a "more nurturing" environment. When Cindy got to high school, Betty always made sure she was on hand to help with registration so that her daughter would get the best teachers and the classes she needed.

Cindy didn't know what to think when her English teacher said: "I'll bet your mother used to dress you in pink clothes and frilly bonnets, didn't she?" Cindy went home that day and asked her mother what the teacher had meant by the question. Betty told her not to worry about it. Betty's protective attitude was exactly what the teacher had been referring to.

About that time (when Cindy was sixteen) her eating disorder began; her bulimia continued for many years. Everyone, especially the Horsely family, was puzzled as to its cause.

One of the mistakes Betty made was trying to protect her daughter from life's bumps and bruises. She didn't realize that if she allowed her daughter to fail at times, Cindy would be more likely to succeed in life. Both Betty and Bob fell into the trap of sexual stereotyping; by withholding affection from Jeff to make him "strong," they actually turned him into a rather insecure young man.

Because Cindy was a girl, they smothered her with more attention than she needed, causing her to feel helpless.

Coping with Feelings

Learning to Love Yourself by Gay Hendricks is a useful book. Hendricks says that many people have troublesome feelings about their parents. Most young people think they must feel only love for their parents when actually they feel anger, fear, gratitude, and other mixed emotions. All of these feelings about parents are normal.

Those coping with an eating disorder must learn to appreciate and celebrate all feelings rather than trying to numb them out. Even feelings considered bad are a normal and an important part of being human.

In the story of Jeff and Cindy, Jeff never got fully in touch with his feelings. His parents misunderstood the purpose of feelings and feared that if Jeff cried over a skinned knee he would never grow up to be a "man." Nothing could be further from the truth. The truth is that to really grow up we have to feel free to express our feelings safely and fully.

Cindy also grew up trying to "stuff" her feelings. She stuffed them down her throat with food; she swallowed them with alcohol, which numbed her out and which she eventually began to overuse. Cindy noticed that some of her friends smoked or exercised excessively. She wondered if that was their way of trying to deal with feelings. Others kept too busy to feel much of anything, or they became involved in compulsive, destructive relationships. These people never learned to trust themselves.

Sometimes, instead of acknowledging and accepting their feelings, people with eating disorders let their feelings overwhelm them. Loneliness, anxiety, the need to please, feeling inadequate—any of these circumstances can trigger a binge in a bulimic or a compulsive eater. An anorexic, instead of experiencing the normal pleasures of living (one of which is eating), is terrified by the prospect of food.

At age nineteen Cindy wrote this in her diary: "I have to get out my anger, so I don't chow tonight. I can hardly stand the tension—finals, weight, my eating problem, my relationships. I feel bad because Walt and I just had an argument over—get this—ice cream. I don't like the way he's started to monitor my eating. The whole thing is so complicated. I know it's because he cares. But it's the same thing my parents try to do. When I told him that, he *really* got angry. I know he gets tired of my complaining—how I feel sick, how my stomach hurts, etc. It's the same thing I do to my mom. He tried to make me stop bingeing, and that hurts my feelings. What I feel next is guilt, my most unfavorite feeling in the whole world. Life is complicated. I couldn't begin to explain all the conflicts."

When Betty told her own mother that Cindy was having a difficult year in college, Cindy's grandma replied, "I just can't understand it—she's had everything."

Had Cindy had everything? Or had she had too much of some things and not enough of others? Perhaps Betty had "smothered" Cindy, preventing her from maturing into a competent person. Maybe her father hadn't paid *enough* attention to her. Who knows? Cindy was right. Life can get complicated.

Sharon Wegscheider-Cruse, who writes about recovery from alcohol addiction, gives the following tips to those learning to appreciate their feelings:

1. Detoxify. In other words, stop using substances such as food, alcohol, or drugs to try to anesthetize your feelings. Become a child again; experience the hurts and allow yourself to feel the joy of being alive.
2. Find a place to let out your old feelings so you can experience your current feelings. Going to a support group or talking with a therapist are both excellent choices.
3. Fill yourself with *new* feelings. Find things to get excited about rather than letting yourself focus on food. Life is full of possibilities. Find healthy ways to have fun. Laugh. Life is not supposed to be all gloom and doom.

Feelings are one of the most important parts of all of us. Not only do we need to learn to live with them, but we should welcome them and learn from them.

CHAPTER 6

The Road to Maturity

W
e have said a lot about the importance of learning to feel our feelings. People with eating disorders often have trouble accepting their feelings, expressing their feelings, or knowing what they really think and feel. John Bradshaw says that you have to express your emotions to gain control over them. If you deny your feelings, "you no longer have your emotions, they have you."

A person with an eating disorder may also be co-dependent and have trouble with various parts of her inner self. Such difficulties may keep a person from growing up and becoming fully mature. Pia Mellody says that these problems include: (1) difficulty with self-esteem; (2) trouble accepting one's own reality; (3) doing things to excess; (4) lacking boundaries; and (5) difficulty taking care of one's own needs.

Self-Esteem: Do I Like Me?

A person who doesn't value himself or herself enough has a problem with self-esteem or self-worth. In her book *Peoplemaking*, Virginia Satir calls this characteristic "high pot" and "low pot." When your self-esteem is high and you feel good about yourself, your pot is full. You have "high pot." At other times you may feel bad about yourself; at those times you have "low pot."

Satir adds that when a person who has low pot much of the time experiences defeats in life (as we all do), that person may feel absolutely desperate. She may ask herself how a person as worthless as she can possibly "cope." Defeated, she may then turn to alcohol, drugs, gambling, overeating, or any number of other such behaviors as a way of trying to make herself feel better.

Satir suggests trying a game around the dinnertable with your family. Tell each other your feelings. Compare the things that make you feel "high pot" or "low pot." That is one way to get emotionally closer to the people with whom you live.

Next, expand the game. Try figuring out what happens to your pot every time someone in the family talks to you. Tell that person. Then, halfway through dinner, start listening to what *you* say to other family members. Imagine what your words do to *their* pot. The next night you can tell your family what you were trying to accomplish by this exercise.

Low self-esteem has many causes. Some people have acquired bad feelings about themselves from their parents, who also have bad feelings about themselves. Actually, parents often pass low-pot messages to their children without realizing what they're doing. Authors Gay and Kathryn Hendricks identify one major problem that people need to solve to get rid of their addictions. They call that problem the "Upper Limits Problem."

Most of us cannot be loving with ourselves for more than a few seconds before we plunge ourselves into pain. Have you ever noticed that when you start feeling good you find something to worry about or another way to make yourself feel bad? The Upper Limits Problem.

The need to solve this problem is especially important for those recovering from addictions. Food, drugs, liquor, sex, shopping—people use these "remedies" to avoid facing deeper problems. Then when the addiction becomes a really *big* problem, the person's energy goes into dealing with *that* problem instead of what the person worried about in the first place (which is, of course, still there). What an unhealthy state of affairs!

An eating disorder can cause you to feel worthless, no good. On the other hand, you may have developed an eating disorder partly as a response to feelings of worthlessness. As an intelligent person, you need to find ways to get out of that vicious circle. Your job is to develop a healthy self-esteem based on belief in yourself as a worthwhile person.

Remember: You are a one-of-a-kind person, and for that reason alone you must learn to value yourself. That is sometimes hard to learn, especially if you have always tied your self-worth to what others think of you.

Some people who seem to have high self-esteem really don't. Their feeling of self-worth comes from the things they own or from positions of power they have over others.

True self-esteem comes from within a person. People with the right amount of self-esteem have found ways to value themselves for the special people they are. No one in the world has quite your combination of characteristics. Let's see how a problem with self-esteem can get people in trouble, and how it can even lead to the development of an eating disorder.

Annie and Cassandra: Opposites Attract?

Annie and Cassandra were best friends through elementary school and high school. Annie was short, chunky, and shy. Cassie was tall, thin, and bossy. When the girls were young they loved writing plays and giving themselves the starring roles. They dressed up in old clothes they found in a trunk in Cassie's basement.

One day the girls decided to do a play for the neighborhood children and charge a quarter admission. Annie's mother, who had low self-esteem herself and had passed the trait to her daughter, didn't think anyone would show up for the play. She hated to see the girls get their hopes up too high. "Probably no one will come," said Annie's mother in her quiet voice.

"We'll make *sure* they'll come," said Cassie's mother in her very loud voice. (Her self-esteem was based largely on things money could buy.) She rushed to the bakery and bought cupcakes and cookies. She told the girls to advertise the fact that "Refreshments Will Be Served."

A large number of neighbor kids assembled. Finally, the curtain rose. The audience members were not very interested in the play, but they loved the refreshments Cassie's mom had bought.

When the girls grew up they went their separate ways. When Annie was eighteen she developed an eating disorder, which, she later discovered, had to do partly with her feelings of low self-worth and her isolation from people. She thought so little of herself that she couldn't stand being around other people. No matter with whom she hung out, she felt inferior. So-and-so was prettier. So-and-so was smarter. So-and-so was richer. Sitting on her bed every evening, Annie munched her way up to 215 pounds. Food was a friend that never judged her; food was always there for her.

Cassie, on the other hand, did not develop an eating disorder, but she did suffer from disillusionment. She had gotten into her mother's habit of buying friendships. She bought clothes for her girlfriends; she took guys out to dinner. Before long, these "store-bought" friends drifted away and left Cassie alone. She felt betrayed and abandoned. When Cassie realized she couldn't buy friends, she became depressed.

How then does a person go about improving her self-esteem? The most important thing is to understand that changing your self-concept may be a slow process, that it may not happen overnight.

The next step is to challenge your beliefs. Do you *really* think a person's self-worth should be based on how much he or she weighs? Challenging such erroneous beliefs can be done with the help of books, a counselor, or a support group.

An advantage of participating in a support group is that you will find others who are struggling with the same issues you are. You will observe that when Suzie Q speaks she sounds intelligent. Perhaps she weighs more than you think she should. That doesn't mean she is less valuable than anyone else. Maybe she's bulimic or anorexic, but you begin to judge on the basis of other qualities. As time goes on, you may be better able to appreciate yourself for *your* valuable qualities.

Another way to improve self-esteem is by trying new experiences. Sometimes you'll fail at what you do, but many other times you'll succeed. Whatever happens, you can give yourself a pat on the back for your effort. Eventually you'll get in the habit of valuing the *process* of trying rather than only the outcome of your attempt.

Jasmine: A for Effort

More than anything in the world, Jasmine wanted to be an actress. Her mother disagreed with the idea. When Jasmine wanted to take drama in her junior year of high school, her mother made her take typing instead. She said typing would be more useful later in life. Nevertheless, Jasmine, a shy girl, got up the courage to audition for the spring musical.

Jasmine didn't even make the chorus. At that point she could have quit trying, but she didn't. Eventually she did get a part in the chorus—in the last semester of her senior year. Remembering an old saying she had heard somewhere, "There are no small parts, only small actresses," Jasmine gave the small part her best shot.

The story had a happy ending. The director of a children's theater company spotted Jasmine and asked her to become a member of his company. But even if Jasmine had never gotten a part in any play, she could have valued herself and her courage in trying.

Besides learning to love our feelings, even angry and sad feelings, we need to love our bodies and our sexuality. Sometimes before we can *love* our bodies, we have to give ourselves permission to *hate* our bodies. Later we can begin to love our physical selves with all of our imperfections.

Many people have been taught that sexual feelings are not okay. Parents fear that their children will act out their sexual feelings, and they therefore try to squelch them. But sexual feelings are a normal, wonderful part of life. Some people, such as those who have been sexually abused, have had unpleasant experiences with sex. Although the past cannot be changed, people can break the grip of their past by making good decisions about the future.

Who Am I?

Many people have trouble accepting their own reality. Experts have noted that this problem with "self-awareness" or difficulty believing in oneself is common among those with eating disorders. People who lack self-awareness wonder, "Who am I?" or "What do I really think?" They look outside themselves for anwers, and they compare themselves (almost always unfavorably) to others.

Annie is a good example. She once said to her journalism teacher, "I could never write editorials because I don't know what I think." Annie felt like a lost soul, unsure of herself and her own reality. Like Loretta with her security blanket, Annie found her comfort in food.

Katherine, a participant in Overeaters Anonymous, said at a meeting, "OA has helped me understand what I'm *not*. My value doesn't come from having a handsome boyfriend or from getting the lead in the spring musical or from being the valedictorian. My value comes from being me."

Ways of coping with a lack of self-awareness are similar to those suggested for increasing self-esteem. Have you ever sat in class knowing an answer but afraid to give it? When someone else offers the same thing you were thinking, the teacher says, "Yes! Wonderful idea." Meanwhile, you're kicking yourself under your desk. Remember, your guess is as good as the next person's and maybe better. Sometimes you'll be wrong; other times you'll be right. Trust yourself.

She Does Everything to Excess!

Those with eating disorders tend to overdo. Bulimics and compulsive eaters eat too much. Anorexics starve too much and often exercise too much. People with eating disorders fear that they won't be able to stop eating once they've started. In an effort to relieve emotional pain, all focus on food.

Annie often starved herself all day, especially if she was going out to dinner that night. Sometimes at the restaurant she ordered gobs of food and then ate very little. That behavior upset her parents, especially her father. (His parents had made him clean his plate.)

One evening during the winter break of her first year of college, Annie went out to dinner with her parents. Late that night when everyone had gone to bed, Annie woke up and crept downstairs to the kitchen. Here's how she described the action:

"I felt this extreme *guilt* for making my poor body digest those huge amounts of heavy food at 4 a.m. while everyone else was snoozing. I was so afraid my dad was going to come stomping down the stairs and scare the heck out of me. Caught in the act! Thank goodness, he didn't. The pressure—it was intense. An hour later I went back upstairs in the darkness. The floor squealed with every step. It was terrible. Finally I was back in my bed, and all I could think about was how I needed a hug."

During her recovery from an eating disorder, Gerry, a compulsive eater, described her excesses this way: "I was like the pendulum of a clock—swinging from one extreme to the other. With me, it was either agony or ecstasy.

Now that I'm well into recovery, I don't need drugs, compulsive sex, or cigarettes. It feels good to be somewhere in the middle all the time. I value myself. Now I know I don't have to be perfect."

Boundaries: Where I Leave Off and You Begin

Boundaries, like fences, help us know what is ours and what is not. A person with strong boundaries can feel sympathy for another person but avoid taking on that person's problems. Boys have an easier time establishing boundaries than girls. A girl may see herself as an extension of her mother (the major caregiver) and wonder where she stops and someone else begins. With her frequent phone calls and incessant demands, Nikki drives every boy she meets out of her picture. Sometimes she does the same thing to her girlfriends. As a result, she has few friends and is often lonely. People who have boundary problems may invade the space of others or let others invade their space.

Annie did both. She made enemies in her own family because of her inability to respect their property. Once when she was expected home from college for a vacation, her brother said, "I wish she wouldn't come. I get tired of locking up all my stuff." Annie's sister had even more of a problem than their brother. Annie helped herself to her sister's clothes, earrings, and cosmetics. Most of the time she didn't bother to ask. Annie didn't know why she took other people's things.

Sometimes bulimics end up stealing food; often they hoard it. Annie's coat pockets bulged with packages of artificial sweetener from restaurants. When she visited her grandmother she selected choice foods from the shelves and took them home in her backpack.

Annie began to realize that her lack of boundaries extended to her relationships outside the family. For example, she "fell in love" too easily. Once a guy she barely knew invited her to move in with him—and she did. In a short time the relationship became destructive. Annie's feelings got hurt. Eventually the guy tired of her and kicked her out. Not only was Annie hurt, she also had no place to live.

Some psychologists link this lack of boundaries to a problem in a child's relationship with early caregivers. In normal relationships a baby cries, and its needs are met. If its needs are not met for some reason, the child may grow up with a lack of trust. Take Kitty, for example.

Kitty: A Colicky Baby

At two months of age Kitty cried almost all of her waking hours. No matter what her mother did to comfort her, Kitty screamed. Her mother had two other children, three and five years old. There was no way, she thought, that she could carry Kitty around all the time. It didn't seem to help anyway. Besides, thought Kitty's mother, if I don't get away from this screaming child I might harm her. It seemed the better choice (after making sure Kitty was fed and dry) to leave her in her crib, close the door to her room, and let her yell.

Today as a fifteen-year-old Kitty has bulimia. Her mother thinks it's all her fault for letting Kitty cry. Although Kitty has not been arrested yet, she has done some shoplifting. She has helped herself to lipstick and perfume on more than one occasion. Perhaps her lack of boundaries resulted from events in her infancy.

Problems with boundaries can also come from abuse. A child who has experienced physical, emotional, or sexual abuse has had her boundaries invaded. As a result, she may feel shame; she may believe that she is somehow to blame. Or she may feel safe and protected only when fat.

Take Care of Whom?

Our culture has always looked favorably on women and girls who take care of others and try hard to please. These same females begin to think that others will care for them in the same way. When that doesn't happen, the person may be disappointed.

Women in our society are expected to be caregivers. Women are overrepresented in the caregiving professions—nursing, social work, teaching. Men expect women to take care of them. In caring for others, however, women may neglect themselves. Certainly, starving oneself is unhealthy; so are bingeing, purging, and massive overeating. And yet overeating may be the only way some women know how to nurture themselves. If they're fat enough, their subconscious minds tell them that they'll have "enough" for themselves *and* for others.

Pat: One Who Cared

Pat, a nursing student, cared for stray animals, she took care of old people at her volunteer job at a nursing home, and she waited on her boyfriend. Worried about going home for spring break, Pat wrote: "Right now I'm at the point where I don't even care anymore, which is a bad feeling to have. I wish I could fall asleep and forget all my troubles. I want to go home, but I have mixed feelings about that too. I wonder if my friends will want to see me—like Joanne, five feet, seven inches, 105 pounds. She makes me sick. I'm jealous, I guess. Me with my huge thighs. No wonder, after what I ate last night—peanut butter, butter, honey, and bananas all mixed together. Cheese, ice cream, cookies. FAT! I hate the word. I'm going to sleep."

Coping with Growing Up

One of the most important steps anyone with an eating disorder can take is admitting that she has a problem not only with food but with emotions and relationships as well. Then what?

The second step is realizing that by making choices each of us has the power to change. The flip side of this second step may be to admit a certain amount of "powerlessness." Those who become part of a twelve-step program admit that they are powerless in relation to food and accept the help of a Higher Power, however they interpret that power. Accepting such authority is not in conflict with any formal religion. Some experts give this advice: Accept the help of a therapist or a group, but don't expect anyone but yourself to do the work of changing yourself. Find which of these approaches works for you and believe in it. And don't forget, too, to believe in yourself.

The third step is taking the *risk* of changing. "Get different," get healthy. Getting help is one such change. First you might try a therapist. You might also find a support group helpful. A twelve-step support group such as Overeaters Anonymous is one kind of supplemental help. This international organization is not just for overweight folks. Anyone who thinks constantly of food (To eat or not to eat—that is the question) is welcome.

An additional note: A person who is not familiar with the concept of "recovery" may make the mistake of asking when and how another person conquered an eating disorder. Why is that a mistake? Because a person may never totally conquer the eating disorder. Some people believe that you *can* recover fully, whereas others consider recovery an ongoing process. Whatever you believe, the best-case scenario is that with the proper help things will keep getting better, and life will become manageable in relation to food and feelings.

Many experts have observed that anorexia often begins when a teenager is moving into adulthood and facing bodily changes. Bulimia most often occurs at a later transition point, such as times of going away to college, moving away from home, or getting married. For those facing such transitions, John Bradshaw's comments should be reassuring: "Growing up means leaving home and becoming a self-supporting adult. I think that is the hardest task any human being has to face."

Is it any wonder that challenged by such difficult tasks, as well as society's pressures, many people develop eating disorders?

CHAPTER 7

Eating Well/Living Well

Forget the quick fix. There isn't one. Some experts say that at any given moment twenty million Americans are dieting. Most dieters (as many as 98 percent) regain their lost weight within five years. And many of those who have tried diets end up on the long treadmill of an eating disorder.

What Works, What Doesn't Work, and Why

You think you're too fat. You should go on a diet. Before you take such a drastic step, talk to your doctor. A doctor will be able to tell you whether or not you are really overweight and if so, how to go on a supervised weight-loss program.

Before you begin a weight-loss program, there are several things to remember:

- If you're somewhere within your ideal weight

range, you probably are not too fat and don't need
to lose weight. (Your doctor has charts that show
ideal weight ranges.)
- The diet industry is big business. Lots of people
would like to hook you into their way of doing
"business." As you *lose* (pounds), they hope to *gain*
(money).
- The cultural standard in this country is "skinny."
Not just thin, but skinny. The trouble with skinny
is that too thin is not too healthy.
- Going on a diet disturbs the person's natural ability
to know how much he or she needs to eat to satisfy
hunger. That interference can be the beginning of
the diet-binge-purge cycle. Diets often turn normal
people into people who fear food.

After reading all that, do you *still* want to diet? If so,
consider the theory of *setpoint*. According to this theory,
everyone has an ideal weight, the person's normal weight
when exercising regularly and eating a balanced diet.
Your setpoint is the weight your genes intended you to
have. Setpoint theory tell us that some "overweight"
people who have reduced by dieting and are always
hungry may actually be "underweight."

Has anyone ever told you, "Eat only when you're
hungry"? If you follow that advice, you should be able to
eat a variety of foods and still maintain a stable weight.

Experts say there are three things you can do with your
setpoint in mind. First, you can live with it and accept
yourself as the wonderful person you are. So what if you
weigh five or ten pounds more than your best friend,
Skinny Minnie?

The second thing you can do about your setpoint is to
try to lower it by exercising more than usual. Although

some people exercise too much, the rest of us probably don't exercise enough. Exercise not only causes a decrease in body fat but also improves a person's mood. "But," you say, "I rode my bike to the pool a couple of times last summer, and I didn't lose weight." Hold it! Don't be in such a hurry. Getting in shape takes months or even years. Studies show that at least two months of training is necessary to reduce body fat, provided the exercise is strenuous enough. Half of Americans don't exercise at all, and half of those who start an exercise program quit within six months.

In *Handbook of Eating Disorders*, authors Stern and Lowney give five tips to help people stick to an exercise program:

1. Find a place to exercise that is conveniently located.
2. Make exercise enjoyable.
   a. Choose activities you like to do.
   b. Vary the type of exercise and the setting.
   c. Make exercise more enjoyable by doing it alone, with another person, or in a group, as you prefer.
3. Don't expect too much too soon. Exercise does not have to hurt to be beneficial. Fitness takes time—think months rather than days.
4. Keep a daily exercise log if that helps, but don't be excessively goal-oriented.
5. Finally, if you have trouble staying with your exercise program, think of some activity that you really *like* to do. Put off the preferred activity until you have exercised.

The third thing you can do about your setpoint is to

diet. This option may be bad for your health and can lead to an eating disorder. Dieting often leads to bingeing. A person who is really obese needs to lose weight gradually over a period of two or three years. The last thing any person needs is a quick weight-loss scheme.

Shannon wrote in her journal: "Thanks to porking out (mainly on the chocolate chip bars Tina made), I've gained almost five gross, nasty, ugly pounds. How in the heck could I have gained that much weight in such a short time? I did eat a lot, but that's incredible! I'm ticked because I worked so hard to lose it. That's why I didn't eat dinner tonight."

Shannon explained later that she had "worked hard" to lose weight by skipping meals. As a result, the chocolate chip bars were especially enticing. Feeling deprived by her diet, Shannon ripped into them. By skipping dinner, she set herself up for another binge.

It is true that anorexics who start eating normally again gain weight. Usually everyone except the person herself thinks she looks much better. It is also true that bulimics who give up vomiting may gain a few pounds at first. The goal of treatment, however, is to help the compulsive person realize that happiness, health, and acceptance of self are much more important than weight.

What Else Doesn't Work

It's amazing the lengths to which people will go to try to lose weight. They begin by thinking they're doing something good for themselves and later realize the harm they may have done to the only body they'll ever have.

Purging by vomiting is the most common thing people with eating disorders do to try to lose weight. They think that this way they can have their cake and get rid of it too.

However, vomiting does not remove all food from the stomach. Therefore, as a result of overeating, people who binge and purge may actually *gain* weight. Another depressing fact for those who have relied on vomiting is that the more they vomit, the less effective the method becomes.

People with eating disorders sometimes use medications advertised to help them lose weight. Any weight loss will be temporary, but the harm done may be permanent.

Diuretics are medicines doctors sometimes prescribe for patients with a heart condition who retain fluid in body tissues because of an inefficient heart pump. People who need diuretics should use them under medical supervision. Diuretics cause the body to lose fluid, but the fluid returns to the tissues as soon as the drug is stopped. These medicines can upset the body's mineral balance. The imbalance may lead to nausea, dizziness, general weakness, and heart irregularities. Constant use of diuretics can actually cause the body to retain water.

Laxatives are totally useless for weight control. By the time food reaches the large intestine, the body has already absorbed most of the calories. Laxative use over a long period of time can cause constipation and loss of bowel tone. Laxatives can also cause gas pains and even tumors of the bowel. Laxatives are medicines. Normal, active young people who eat a healthy diet, including fruits, vegetables, and grains, don't need laxatives and shouldn't take them. Like diuretics, laxatives draw water, as well as necessary minerals, from the body. Any weight loss caused by laxative abuse will be temporary. The damage done, however, may be permanent.

Emetics are substances that cause vomiting. Syrup of ipecac is an emetic as well as a very dangerous drug. Doctors sometimes prescribe it for children who have mistakenly swallowed a harmful substance. Ipecac causes vomiting, but it is intended only as a way of getting rid of poisons, not food. When it builds up in the body, it can cause death.

In addition to the dangers associated with each of the above substances, combinations of them can be life-threatening.

CHAPTER 8

Everything Else You've Always Wanted to Know . . .

Are Eating Disorders Dangerous?

Yes! First, anorexia. The most obvious danger, of course, is starvation. Because the person with anorexia nervosa has a distorted view of her body, she sees herself (or parts of herself) as too fat even when she may be starving herself to death. Relatives are not likely to stand by and watch someone they love die of starvation; therefore, the person may have to be hospitalized and force-fed.

Marcia: Lucky to Be Alive

Talk to Marcia today, and you'll hear a young woman who feels lucky to be alive. As she balances her two-year-old daughter on one knee and her four-year-old son on the other, Marcia recalls her anorexic days. "I was eighteen when my father died and Mom went back to work," she says. "I'm the middle child, the oldest girl, and I had to take care of my little sister every day until Mom got home. We amused ourselves by fixing food. And eating food. I stuffed myself till I thought I'd burst; I felt like a blimp. When Mom got home from work, she'd be tired and crabby. I couldn't wait to move out.

"When I was twenty, I joined this religious cult; that's where I met my husband-to-be. The marriage didn't last—neither did the cult's appeal, and I split. When I moved back home I saw what a porker I was. I just stopped eating. Gradually I went down to seventy pounds, and I'm five feet, four inches. I got so weak I couldn't *crawl* around the house. They put me in the hospital and wouldn't let me out until I weighed a hundred pounds, but the minute I got out I'd start losing again. I had this little potbelly like a starvation victim, half of my hair fell out, and my wrists looked like match sticks. But I still *felt* fat."

Her mother adds, "I hated to see her in a swimming suit. Her bones stuck out like chicken wings, but she still exercised constantly. She had a stationary bike, where she sat pedaling away until she almost dropped. If friends came over, they had to talk to her while she rode . . . and rode . . . and rode. Finally, she didn't have any friends. When she wasn't exercising she was boiling vegetables—carrots and celery, that was all she ate. She cooked those vegetables and rode that damn bike until I was sure she was going to die. She was in and out of the hospital eight or ten times."

"I don't know what did it," says Marcia. "Finally I had just had enough. I heard of people who had died from my disease—people my age with families—and I didn't want

to die . . . " Her voice trails off. "Maybe I realized I'd sat
on that bike long enough."

Statistics vary, but a reliable estimate is that up to 10
percent of anorexics ultimately die from their disease.
One life-threatening complication of anorexia is irregular
heartbeat. Others are constipation; dull, stringy hair that
falls out in clumps; dry skin; and a growth of fine, animal-
like hair ("lanugo") over the body. Vitamin C deficiency
can cause weakened gum tissues. A lack of salivary fluid in
the mouth may cause dental caries (cavities).

Bulimia also presents dangers. Although not as many
people die, and bulimics often appear normal, victims can
die of heart complications and other problems related to
the disease. Throwing up gets rid not only of food but also
other substances the body needs. Vomiting can damage
the enamel of the teeth, resulting in numerous cavities as
well as swollen salivary glands. The cheeks become puffy,
and the person looks a bit like a chipmunk. Acid from the
stomach can also damage the esophagus.

April, a recovering bulimic, says that she became aware
of her eating disorder during her college days. April was a
pre-med perfectionist who wanted to get straight As. She
studied hard and put herself under a lot of stress. She
justified her occasional purging to herself and family by
claiming that she had a "nervous stomach."

Other people with eating disorders may admit having a
problem but be unable to stop their self-destructive behavior. In such instances the condition has become an
addiction. Knowledge of the dangers can be a first step
toward recovery.

Penny: A Disappearing Act

Penny had always considered herself chunky. The boys she liked never liked her. Only the other girls and the male geeks paid any attention to her. In her junior year of high school Penny joined every activity she could—choir, yearbook, newspaper staff, drama club. She swam on the swim team and played soccer. Penny knew that being in lots of activities was the path to popularity.

Penny wanted to be a cheerleader, but she messed up in the tryouts. She ran for student council vice-president and lost. She began to think something must be terribly wrong with her. (It didn't occur to her that most people who try for things have an equal failure rate.)

Penny decided that she must be too fat. She stopped eating breakfast and lunch. She ate dinner but usually got around to only a few bites of meat and salad. Penny lost forty pounds. Her periods stopped. Finally her mother took her to the pediatrician who had known her all her life. Penny reacted to the stricken look on the doctor's face when he saw her. "My friend," he said, "you are soon going to disappear. Don't you want to live?"

Penny *did* want to live. She wanted to go to the Homecoming game even if she had to go with the girls. She wanted to write for the school newspaper even if some of her stories were rejected. She wanted to go to college. Penny didn't want to disappear. She began to drink milkshakes for breakfast and to eat rather normally again. Eventually her menstrual periods returned.

Now twenty-eight years old and happily married, Penny wants to have a family. After trying for two years, she hasn't succeeded in getting pregnant.

Might Penny's time of self-starvation during adolescence have anything to do with her possible infertility?

Physicians are not sure whether starvation during the teenage years affects fertility in later life, but all would agree that eating a balanced diet is best.

Sharing

People with eating disorders seem to share many traits. Anorexics starve while bulimics and compulsive eaters eat too much. People with eating disorders tend to do things to excess. In addition, some share the characteristic of body-image distortion. This is like looking at yourself in the fun house mirror. Most people laugh about that image, but the activity wouldn't be enjoyable if they considered the image real. Anorexics see themselves as too fat when they are actually too skinny. A compulsive eater may see herself as normal when she is in fact quite overweight.

People with eating disorders also share a tendency to have compulsive personalities. Donna Gilbert-Pierce, a therapist, says that clients rarely have only one addictive disorder; more often they have several compulsions or addictions. For example, when a person gets her eating problems under control, excessive drinking may surface. The person may become addicted to cigarettes, or to television, or to compulsive spending. The person may become a workaholic or a compulsive gambler, jogger, or golfer. It is not unusual for participants in an Overeaters Anonymous group to have also participated in Alcoholics Anonymous or Narcotics Anonymous.

Celeste: Hiding

Celeste, whose anorexia led to bulimia, says, "My thoughts focused on how to avoid eating. I feared social situations that included food. I lied to get out of going to restaurants with friends. I felt powerful when I ate less. I smoked cigarettes to avoid eating. I thrived on hearing comments regarding my weight. I feared criticism from others concerning my actions. At night I binged on snack foods, then purged."

Gilbert-Pierce believes that until a person gets into a twelve-step program or other support group in which she learns to love herself, her compulsions will turn into addictions. She believes that any treatment for an eating disorder has to focus on the compulsive nature of the disorder.

One reason addictions sometimes occur in clumps is that the person, looking for solutions to problems, gets a temporary "high" from the addictive behavior. Too bad that the high lasts only a short time before it becomes a low. Then the cycle starts all over again.

Anorexics get a high from the control they imagine that they gain over food, as well as over people. Later they realize that they are not in control but are *being* controlled by food and thoughts of food.

People with eating disorders also seem to share other personality traits. We know that eating disorders have no one cause and no one cure. Similarly, the experts say that no personality type is shared by all people with eating disorders. Nevertheless, certain characteristics seem to be more common in those with certain conditions.

Anorexics are often shy, conscientious, competitive, and perfectionistic. In other words, they tend to be rather "uptight." They may also lack self-confidence and fear growing up.

Bulimics are more likely to be impulsive, depressed,

prone to compulsions or addictions, and emotionally troubled. They often have low self-esteem and problems with relationships. Sometimes, however, it is hard to figure out which caused what. Did depression contribute to the eating disorder, or did the eating disorder cause depression?

Crossing the Line

In *Fat Is a Family Affair*, Judi Hollis talks about crossing the invisible line from compulsion to addiction. A compulsion is an irresistible urge to do something that may be harmful. But an addiction is worse. Addictions consume, making normal living impossible. If a person cannot stop a behavior, he or she is addicted. Bulimics and compulsive eaters cannot stop eating. Anorexics cannot *start* eating for fear they won't be able to stop.

Nadia: Chaos

Nadia, twenty-seven, lives in Bloomington, Indiana. Her parents live in nearby Indianapolis. One day Sarah, a former high school classmate, called Nadia's parents. She wanted to get in touch with her old friend to tell her about their tenth class reunion. Nadia's mother had to look up her daughter's number. Nadia moves so often that her mom never has a chance to learn her address and phone number.

Over the years Nadia has had girl housemates and guy housemates and sometimes both. (Nadia's parents have always paid her rent because Nadia can't afford it. If she lives at home, the family and the house get "torn up.") No matter who Nadia's housemates are, they always end up forcing her to move. Her weird eating habits are too much. She eats the roommates' food during midnight binges. The kitchen is always a mess, and so is the bathroom.

Nadia seems much younger than her twenty-seven years. She acts and looks seventeen. For her birthday she asked that her mother and father take her out to dinner. She also asked that they *not* bring her sister or brother along. With a laugh she admitted that she had never felt she received enough of her parents' attention. (Nadia's sister is twenty-six; her brother is twenty-four.)

Nadia bounces from one waitressing job to another. Her employers become as exasperated with her as her housemates do. Nadia loses most of her jobs because she comes in late for work after bingeing or drinking (or both) much of the night and being unable to get up in the morning. Sometimes she steals food or money from the restaurant; occasionally she steals from other places. Nadia smokes a pack of cigarettes a day. She latches onto various boyfriends and smothers them with her neediness.

Although she loves her daughter with all her heart, Nadia's mother tries not to call her too often. She thinks it's time for Nadia to grow up. She feels guilty about whatever they did wrong in raising her. Perhaps they overprotected her. Nadia's father feels guilty too. Whenever Nadia can't pay her bills, he sends money.

Nadia feels sad and confused, almost desperate. She knows she'll be sorry if she misses her class reunion; she used to be very close to some of those people. On the other hand, she fears she'll be equally sorry if she goes. She'll compare herself unfavorably to all the "successful" people there. She'll feel fat, and she'll no doubt eat, drink, and smoke too much. Nadia knows that her life is out of control, but she can't seem to do a thing about it.

*   *   *

In the first place. Nadia does not yet understand that her compulsions are running (and ruining) her life. She also is not aware that as she gets rid of one addiction, another one rears its ugly head. Nadia's parents do not fully understand their part in their daughter's eating disorder. By becoming involved as codependents (for example, sending Nadia money when she is perfectly able to earn her own), they are enabling the destructive process to continue.

What Are Binges Like?

No one can describe a typical binge because there is no such thing. Binges are as different as the people who engage in them. Some people are so compulsive that they choose the same foods every time. Others are more imaginative. Especially prized as binge foods are soft, sweet things that go down and come up easily. Ice cream is a real winner. Crystal always binges on vanilla ice cream, butterscotch pudding, and cheesecake. Marcy is compulsive in a different way. She is so worried about calories that she binges only on raw vegetables. A week ago Marcy got a new job. She is stressed to the max. At work she lives on black coffee. Every day after her fifteen-minute bike ride home she bursts in the door of her apartment and consumes pounds of raw cauliflower with ranch dressing. Other bingers are not so selective. They toss down anything they can find in the cupboard or refrigerator.

Many experts believe that binges are a misguided attempt at self-care. Remember Annie? Annie realized that something other than food was missing in her life when she wrote: "Finally, I was back in my bed, and all I could think about was how I needed a hug."

Why Do Anorexics Sometimes Become Bulimic?

No one knows for sure why one eating disorder sometimes follows another, but a person who does not allow herself normal meals is more likely to "blow it" once she again has access to food. That is one reason diets don't work.

A study by Ancel Keys and colleagues at the University of Minnesota more than forty years ago helps us understand why anorexia often leads to bulimia. The researchers restricted the calories of thirty-six healthy young men who had volunteered to participate in the study as an alternative to serving in the military. During the first three months the men ate normally while the researchers noted their behaviors, personalities, and eating patterns. For the next six months they were allowed to eat only half the amount they ate before. They lost on average 25 percent of their original body weights. For the last three months of the study the men again ate what and however much they wanted.

As a result of starvation, most of the men experienced physical, psychological, and social changes. Many became intensely preoccupied with food, not only during the starvation period but afterward as well. For example, three of the men became chefs and one went into the field of agriculture. During the starvation phase the volunteers spent much of their time deciding how they would eat their daily allotment of food. Some gulped their rations while others took two hours to eat a meal. Some made strange concoctions by mixing various food items together, and the use of salt and spices increased dramatically. One man chewed forty packs of gum a day. Because many of the volunteers drank excessive amounts of coffee and tea, their consumption had to be limited to nine cups per day.

One man rummaged through garbage cans trying to find extra food. Even when the starvation period ended, many of the men continued to make weird food combinations or to lick their plates and neglect their table manners.

Looking back at the results of the study, we see behaviors remarkably resembling bulimia. One man, who worked in a grocery store, completely lost his "willpower" and stuffed himself with cookies, a sack of popcorn, and two overripe bananas before getting control of himself. Afterward he suffered from nausea, vomiting, and self-criticism.

Some of the men had weekend splurges during which they ate enormous amounts of food and were unable to stop eating even when they wanted to.

For as long as twelve weeks after the starvation period, many of the men complained of increased hunger immediately after or within an hour after the last meal.

Although the subjects chosen for this experiment were psychologically healthy before the study, many reported emotional changes such as depression after the study. Subjects also reported irritability, angry outbursts, and anxiety. Some men started smoking or biting their nails or both. One man went on a shoplifting spree.

Most of the men were quite social to begin with but later became withdrawn, losing their sense of humor. One man wrote in his diary that he was one of the few who continued to date. He reported, however, that when he took a girl to a movie it required an effort to hold her hand. To him the most interesting parts of movies were scenes that showed people eating.

In addition, the volunteers experienced numerous physical changes, including loss of hair, decreased tolerance to cold, insomnia, stomach upsets, dizziness, and headaches. As they regained weight, their body fat increased, and the men began to worry about "feeling fat." What does all this mean? The Minnesota experiment is important because it shows that many of the symptoms experts thought were specific to either anorexia or bulimia are instead *caused by* starvation. In some cases depression may be a cause of an eating disorder. When we consider the results of Keys's study, however, we find that in many cases anorexia led to bulimia and depression resulted.

Another important finding from the study is that each person has a normal body weight (*i.e.*, the setpoint theory). In the months following the study the volunteers did not gain tremendous amounts of weight. Most gained back their original weight plus 10 percent; then in the next six months their weight gradually returned to normal.

Pam: A College Student and Her Diary

Many bulimics are anorexic all day. Alone at night, they gorge. Some people can avoid binges all week while at work or school, only to let themselves go on weekends. For others, drinking alcohol lowers their inhibitions against compulsive eating. They drink a beer or a glass of wine and "it's all over."

Pam, a college student living in her own apartment, went to the campus health center to get help with her bulimia. The counselor told her to rcord her binges and the feelings that went with them. Here are two of her journal entries:

"Friday, 2:30 a.m.—I ate way too much tonight (and drank too much too). First at Curt's house: nachos, pretzels, three beers, and two glasses of V-8 juice. Then 'dinner.' Peanut butter, cottage cheese, and ice cream. Then a bowl of mushrooms with bleu cheese dressing and a cheese sandwich. Now it's the middle of the night, and I just made a huge bowl of popcorn. (I used a whole container of Parmesan cheese plus a stick of margarine.) Ugh! How disgusting. I feel sick."

"Tuesday, 9 p.m.—Elaine just came over to talk, but I didn't feel like making conversation. All I can think about is how much my stomach is pooching out of my nightgown, and how my thighs touch when I stand in front of the mirror, and how I should be out running. At the same time I feel like lying around and wallowing in my misery. I think I'll go to sleep. (I didn't get up until noon today.) I woke up three times last night to eat—ice cream, granola, Grape Nuts, two bananas, blueberry yogurt, and seven butter-and-salami sandwiches. Why do I do this to myself?"

Can Eating Disorders Be Cured?

Most experts agree that about a third of persons with eating disorders recover completely, another third get somewhere between a little better and a lot better, and the final third don't get much better for a long time, if at all. We do know that no doctor can predict the course of an eating disorder the way a physican might be able to say, "It's chicken pox; it will be gone in about a week." Experts agree that the younger the person and the sooner the eating disorder is treated, the better the success rate.

In *Eating Without Fear*, Lindsey Hall says that bulimia can be cured. But her survey of 213 women with bulimia showed that only 14 percent considered themselves cured while 83 percent reported they were still "in recovery."

Hall admits that at least for a while a compulsive person recovering from an eating disorder may have to rely on some other activity, such as exercise, to distract herself from eating. In time, though, that need will pass.

Compulsive eaters who are participants in the twelve-step program of Overeaters Anonymous consider themselves in recovery; some report that they plan to attend OA meetings for the rest of their lives. As Lillie put it, "Why would I want to stop coming? I've gone to both OA and AA. People ask me, 'How do you have time to go to a meeting every day?' And I say to them, 'Hey, I used to spend a lot more time bingeing, purging, buying binge foods, and sitting in bars than I do now going to meetings."

How Long Will It Last?

An eating disorder will continue until the person decides to take the risk of letting go of the disorder. That is not an easy process, especially for someone who has had anorexia or bulimia for a long time or whose disease is severe. Doctors and therapists have found younger people with anorexia easier to treat than older clients. An older person with bulimia who has binged and purged for years may find recovery more difficult than one who has only occasional binges. Strange as it may seem, food or the disorder itself may have become a friend. This dependable, though destructive, friend may have chased away all of the person's former friends.

The person with an eating disorder may find herself lonely and without supports. For various reasons she may resist help. Sometimes people like the attention their disorder brings. They have become the focus of family concern. Or a person may become so used to feeling depressed and bad about herself that any other feeling doesn't fit. As one participant in a support group observed, "Recovery is making the outside fit with the inside."

Olivia: Unready

Olivia's eating disorder began during the last half of her senior year in high school. Mealtimes were battle times at her house. Before dinner Olivia picked a fight with anyone in the family so she wouldn't have to eat, or she stormed away from the table without eating anything. In the middle of the night she raided the refrigerator.

In college Olivia went to a therapist, who recommended an eating disorder support group. Olivia attended one meeting. "The room was full of sickos," she told her therapist. "One lady weighed less than a match stick, and another one looked like a bag lady." A friend of Olivia's mother urged her to attend a meeting of Overeaters Anonymous in her college town. Olivia agreed but then could never seem to find the meeting place. When she finally did get to a meeting, she complained afterward that most of those attending were "too old."

Olivia's disease stuck to her like a piece of bubble gum on a hot day. Her behavior suggests that she is not ready for treatment. A person who wants to find reasons for not accepting help can always find them. But an untreated eating disorder is likely to get worse. Resources are out there; all you have to do is find them and use them.

CHAPTER 9

Getting Better

A psychologist recently spoke to ninety women (and three men) on the subject of eating disorders. During the break two women approached the speaker.

"I have bulimia," said the younger woman, "and I don't know what to do about it." Tears rolled down her cheeks.

"You're doing an important thing right now," said the speaker. "Being open about your eating disorder is the first step toward recovery." She put a hand on the young woman's shoulder. "How long have you been bulimic?"

"I'd guess about six months."

The psychologist nodded. "Your chances for recovery are excellent. Six months isn't such a long time."

"It feels like forever," said the young woman.

"You're in high school?" asked the psychologist.

"She just graduated," said the girl's mother. "She's going to college in the fall."

Further conversation revealed that the young woman was planning to attend a large university about an hour from home.

As other participants crowded around with their questions, the speaker gave this advice: "Resources will be available through the health service on campus. Get help. Otherwise, you could ruin your whole college life—the way I did." The speaker then told her story. After suffering with bulimia for ten years, including her four years of college, she had had ten "wonderful" years of recovery.

Goals

No matter what your eating disorder and no matter what your treatment, you will be better off in the long run if you first consider some treatment goals.

Goal Number One: Stop! First, if possible, find a way to stop your unhealthy eating habits. Using food to meet your emotional needs may give you the illusion of being in control when actually you're not. Those who believe that eating disorders are an addiction say that as long as the behavior continues, recovery will elude you. As long as you continue to binge and purge, for example, you will be caught in the clutches of the eating disorder.

Remember that starvation itself causes strange behaviors that are beyond a person's control. For example, Ardath's mother reports that when her daughter's weight dropped below eighty pounds she acted like a zombie and started hoarding pizza crusts and boxes of cake mix in her room.

One mistake many people make is thinking that they can stop self-destructive behaviors alone any time they want to. Without help, people have suffered from an eating disorder for ten, twenty, or even thirty years with the misconception: "Tomorrow I'll stop." Almost impossible. You need the support of others. Twelve-step programs suggest taking one step at a time, one day at a time to recovery. Some people have found that taking one *hour* at a time makes life more manageable.

Some experts suggest that compulsive eaters can learn to eat when they're hungry and eat as much as they want. In that way they learn to trust their own body signals and to develop a "normal" relationship with food.

Goal Number Two: Increase Your Self-Esteem. Replace the destructive behaviors and negative self-messages with positive thoughts and healthy behaviors. That is much easier said than done. After years of putting yourself down, it is not easy to start being kind to yourself.

Candice, for example, couldn't accept a compliment. "Candice, what a pretty outfit," said an older woman at church. Candice couldn't bring herself to say "Thank you" and then shut up. Instead, she shrugged and said, "It's just an old hand-me-down from my sister."

Because such bad habits are so ingrained, you will be more successful if you work on bucking yourself up with the help of at least one other person, such as a therapist. You can try to do it alone, guided by book exercises, but the process will be hard, and you may become discouraged. You don't want discouragement; you want success.

Here's another example. Have you ever said something like this to a person? "You big fat ugly slob. You never do anything right."

"Of course not," you reply. "I wouldn't say something like that to my worst enemy." And yet some people speak to *themselves* in a similar way every day of their lives. Give yourself a break. Learn to treat yourself as a friend. After all, you are (or will want to become) your own best friend. If you don't treat yourself with kindness, how can you expect other people to do so?

Try this exercise. Listen to your inner voice or your "self-talk" for three straight days. What do you say to yourself while in the shower? What do you say to your face when looking in the mirror? Do your negative messages to yourself outweigh the positive? If so, it's time for a change.

Do this. Replace all the negative self-talk with affirmations. Affirmations tell you of your own goodness and uniqueness. Make lists of your good points and all that has been right with your life so far. See, it's a long list, isn't it? If not, haven't you forgotten something?

Another thing you may need to learn is to "re-parent" yourself. You may be looking for nurturing from parents who are unable to supply it. As children, they themselves may not have received proper nurturing. Their own parents may have been alcoholic or workaholic; they may have been emotionally, physically, or sexually abused; they may have died or been divorced when your parents were young. Accepting the fact that your parents were not perfect and their lives not ideal may be disappointing or disillusioning, but realizing the truth is not disloyalty to your parents.

Sometimes before people can move toward recovery they have to remember and accept the parts of their lives that were less than good. Sometimes those memories are so painful and deeply buried that they are hard to bring to the surface. That is when professional help can be useful. Failing to acknowledge reality, however, may stand in the way of recovery.

To sum up, we need to learn to be good to ourselves. Remember that there are many ways to be nice to yourself besides eating or keeping yourself from eating. In the past, women have given to others but not to themselves. Start giving to yourself now. You deserve it.

Goal Number Three: Understand the Meaning of Fat in Our Society. If you understand the many meanings of fat/thin in our culture, you will have gone a long way toward understanding yourself. When a person tries to escape problems by focusing on food/fat issues, she is using an unhealthy coping mechanism. According to Geneen Roth in *Feeding the Hungry Heart*, "Fat becomes your protection from anything you need protection from: men, women, sexuality (blossoming or developed), frightening feelings of any sort; it becomes your rebellion, your way of telling your parents, your lovers, the society around you, that you don't have to be who they want you to be. Fat becomes your way of talking. It says: I need help, go away, come closer, I can't, I won't, I'm angry, I'm sad. It becomes your vehicle for dealing with every problem you have."

We could say the same thing about thin (as in anorexia nervosa). A person who uses thinness to measure her self-worth can never be thin enough. She can never be good enough. That is why her goal is to get thinner, and thinner, and thinner . . .

The National Association to Advance Fat Acceptance (NAAFA) is a nonprofit organization of about three thousand people in the United States and Canada. Its aim is to spread the word that everyone, regardless of weight, has a right to dignity and happiness. Barbara Altman Bruno, a social worker who helps people with weight problems, says that people are meant to be different sizes and shapes "like vegetables." Bruno's goal is to help people to separate their self-worth from their weight and to break the cycle of "yo-yo" dieting. She says that women in our society are still valued more for how they look than what they do, even though that has begun to change as women become more prominent professionally and less reliant on a man for their identity.

Goal Number Four: Learn to Eat Again. Your fourth goal is to retrain yourself in healthful eating habits. Again, you will need help. A person with the initials R.D. after his or her name is a registered dietitian accredited by the American Dietetic Association and should be able to help you make a nutrition plan. Those who work daily with people who have eating disorders have found the following tips useful.

One of the most useful things people can do is to commit themselves to three meals a day. No matter what the eating disorder, this can be a useful plan. In Overeaters Anonymous the concept is called "abstinence" and is one of the tools of recovery. The dictionary defines abstinence as "the willful avoidance of pleasures, especially food and drink, thought to be harmful." Naturally, no one can pledge to do without food the way an alcoholic can do without liquor. We have to eat.

With the help of a nutritionist, a person can make and stick to a "meal plan." This plan can take a person a long way toward learning to eat correctly. The three meals are worked out in advance, sometimes with the addition of one or two planned snacks, and the person does not deviate from the plan.

For a compulsive eater, abstinence may mean three meals a day with no snacks. Like the alcoholic who cannot stop drinking after the first compulsive drink, the bulimic or compulsive eater may not be able to stop snacking once she starts. And being unable to stop eating is the anorexic's greatest fear. Therefore, committing oneself to three meals a day can be a step in the right direction.

Another reason for eating three or even four smaller meals is that the body burns more calories when they are spaced throughout the day than when they are contained in one large meal. Also, the spacing of meals reduces hunger, and therefore the tendency to binge. A study done by Weight Watchers showed how skipping meals contributed to binge eating. Thirteen percent of those who ate three meals a day binged, 25 percent of breakfast skippers binged, and 60 percent of those who skipped both breakfast and lunch binged.

A person with an eating disorder may also have to relearn correct portion sizes. Americans tend to think "more is better." When eating out, they like to get their money's worth. The nutritionist may recommend a food scale for weighing portions of meat or cheese and measuring cups for pasta and rice. Once good eating habits are established, such assistance may not be needed.

Therapists and nutritionists advise other behavioral changes associated with eating. Sit down for meals (try not to eat on the run), and eat in the same place whenever possible. (That is similar to the rule about studying in the same place every day.) Let's face it. If you're eating only three squares a day, you'll want to make each meal a wonderful occasion—if you can. Carmen, a secretary in a small business office, usually has to eat lunch alone, yet she often brings a pretty placemat and a fresh flower to put on her desk at lunchtime. Although this embellishment would hardly be possible in the school cafeteria, the point is to enjoy *where* you're eating, not only *what* you're eating. "But," you say, "how can I enjoy the surroundings of the school cafeteria?" Not possible? Then try to find something to enjoy about the people you're with.

Some people believe that sugar triggers binges; if that seems true in your case, eat sugar only with meals or avoid it whenever you can. Other people discover that eliminating sugar not only is impossible but seems to have the opposite effect, making them crave the forbidden treats even more. Such people may have more success allowing themselves a small portion of "forbidden foods." Do what seems to work for you.

Do you think in terms of "bad" foods and "good" foods?

Peanut butter is bad; lettuce is good. Ice cream is bad; broccoli is good. If so, you're not alone. A recent Gallup poll showed that more than two thirds of those surveyed chose foods based on their reputation—good vs. bad. Thirty-six percent of those polled felt guilty about eating the "bad" foods they liked.

Most nutritionists maintain that no foods should be forbidden. They think you can learn to eat anything you want. Some people eliminate entire food groups, such as milk or meat, from their diet as being "fattening." What is important to health, however, is a nutritionally sound diet over a long period of time. Most of us are better off eating some of all kinds of foods, especially important foods such as milk.

A person who lives on her own may find that meal planning and shopping is a way of "having the right things in her basket." Gail, a participant in an eating disorder support group, decided that she hadn't made much progress in three months. "But," she said, "the last time I went to the store I knew things were definitely getting better. When I looked in my shopping cart, I had all the right things."

Buying small quantities of food in individual packets helps some people and does nothing for others. Find what works for you. One compulsive eater found that brushing her teeth with lots of toothpaste right after a meal cut down on her urge to eat again soon. Other techniques people use are taking a walk as soon as they get up from the table or calling a friend as a distraction from thoughts of food or an urge to vomit.

Some experts believe that we need a new way of thinking about food and the meaning of food. In *Breaking Free from Compulsive Eating*, Roth says that people who learn to nurture themselves "break free" from the "shoulds" and "oughts" of dieting. Given a chance, the body knows when it's hungry and what it wants to eat.

Roth gives this advice to bingers:

- Give yourself permission to binge. In that way you can start tasting the food and relaxing about it. If you don't like the taste of what you're eating, you can give yourself permission to stop.
- Don't try to pretend that you're not eating. If you accept the fact that you are bingeing, you might decide to stop.
- Notice the texture, taste, and temperature of the food. Notice how it feels in your mouth, throat, stomach. Maybe it doesn't feel good; maybe it does. Either way, you can decide whether you want to continue to binge. If you like it, keep going. If not, stop.
- In the middle of a binge, go look at your face in the mirror. Touch your face and mouth. Look into your eyes and smile. Remind yourself that you are more than a mouth. Then return to the food if you still want to.
- Talk out loud. Talk to the food. Tell it what it's supposed to be doing for you. Do you want it to make you numb? Put you to sleep? Make you forget about something that happened today?
- If someone walks in during your binge and asks what you're doing, say that you're eating (or bingeing) and invite him or her to join you.
- Afterward be kind to yourself; do something nice for yourself. Analyze the experience you just had. Don't deprive yourself of food the next day. Just eat again when you're hungry.

Therapists and nutrition counselors often advise clients to keep a journal. Recording the feelings and circumstances surrounding a binge may help cut down on the need for binges.

And stay away from that scale! Most professionals agree that weighing once a week is more than enough; others recommend only monthly confrontations with the scale. The 1990 slogan of Eating Disorders Awareness Week was "Being thin is not the answer . . . don't weigh your self-esteem." The recommendation was, "Put away, throw away, or pulverize your scale."

Most of the weight loss in the early stages of a diet is from loss of water. After the initial period the dieter is often depressed because she isn't losing weight fast enough. The point is that self-worth should not be tied to pounds gained or lost. As a person learns to feel better about herself, normal eating behavior will result.

What Is "Normal" Eating?

After years of struggling with weird food habits, many people don't know what "normal" eating is. Further, people with eating disorders tend to sort foods into the previously mentioned "good" and "bad" categories. By eating small amounts of a wide variety of foods, a person is more likely to get over the need to binge.

Teens need between 1,500 and 2,500 calories a day just to keep going. Divided into categories, a day's allotment could include three servings of fruit; three or four servings of low-fat dairy products; six or seven servings of starchy foods; and one or two servings of foods high in iron, such as dark meat of turkey, mature beans, lean beef, lean pork, or chicken. There is no limit on low-calorie vegetables such as celery, carrots, tomatoes, cauliflower, broccoli, green peppers, cabbage, lettuce, mushrooms, or green beans.

The Stress Mess

People with eating disorders often put themselves under unnecessary stress. They are likely to be perfectionists who expect too much from themselves. Or they may have such low self-esteem that no matter what they do, it isn't enough; they always feel bad about themselves. They may be people who take care of others to the neglect of themselves. A person under stress during the day may turn out to be a nighttime binger.

What are your stressors? For some, even the idea of writing a research paper can trigger a binge. Others put themselves under so much stress that they avoid sleep; then they have to eat and drink constantly to have enough energy to keep going. Some people who live away from home find that a trip to their parents' house plays tricks with their thoughts and actions. Going "back home" brings up all sorts of old feelings about love and nourishment. Knowing what to expect enables a person to plan ways to keep from falling into old traps.

Another useful strategy is to find ways to relieve stress. Let's face it—we live in a stress-producing culture. For some, meditation can be a major stress reliever. Meditation is a way of calling a halt to outside pressures and going within to center yourself. A helpful book is *Meditations and Inspirations* by Virginia Satir.

Allow yourself fifteen or twenty minutes a day for each session. Permit no distractions during this time. Lie down or sit in a quiet, comfortable place. Close your eyes and become aware of your breathing—slowly in, slowly out. Your breath comes from the center of your being. Feel the center of your being. Be aware of your breath—let it come from deep inside you. Remind yourself of your need to nurture yourself with all your goodness and all your faults.

Remember a time and place when you felt totally comfortable. Perhaps you'll remember a time on the beach with the waves lapping at your toes, or a hike in the mountains where the air was pure and crisp. Remember a person with whom you felt connected, or think of your connection to the universe. Contemplate your sameness to others and your differentness from others.

Get in touch with your feelings and value each of those feelings as an important part of wonderful you. Keep remembering to breathe slowly and deeply. Allow yourself to appreciate your problems, which help make you truly alive. Perhaps the glimmer of a solution will come to you. If not, don't worry. Let yourself relax and understand that you have choices. You will make good ones and you will make bad ones. That's okay. You are learning to live and be human.

When you are ready, open your eyes and come back to your life, the here-and-now of your existence. Love it; appreciate the gift of life.

You can find many other ways to relax. The main thing to remember is the need to do it. If you find yourself tensing up, stop and breathe deeply. In learning to relax, you are free to use your imagination. What is relaxing for one person (rock music?) may be stress-producing torture for another. Figure out your favorite ways of relaxing and do them. Take a swim, a walk, or a shower; play a game of tennis or chess. Missy likes to relax by brushing the dog; Carrie likes to wash walls.

Help!

Knowing the goals and principles underlying therapy is useful in pointing directions to recovery. Knowing goals, however, is not enough; a person with an eating disorder needs help.

Eating disorder specialists may be medical doctors or mental health counselors such as psychologists or social workers. A medical doctor, especially one with expertise in treating eating disorders, is one of the best persons to assess the situation and rule out physical causes. After considering all the factors, the specialist will make a treatment plan. He or she can then refer the person to the appropriate treatment.

Beth: A Rare Case

Beth's huge dark eyes stared out of sunken sockets. Over a period of two years the ten-year-old had gradually lost weight. During that time her parents took her to their family doctor. He investigated her for a bowel disorder and found nothing wrong. Also during that period Beth's parents separated and considered divorce. A second doctor suspected the marital trouble as the cause of Beth's weight loss. A later and more thorough investigation at a center showed a brain tumor to be the cause.

A circumstance such as Beth's is rare: Although cases of anorexia nervosa seem to be surfacing at much earlier ages, an eating disorder beginning at age eight would be unusual. When an eating disorder is unlikely but still possible, an extensive medical workup may be necessary.

How Do I Find Someone to Help Me?

One of the most useful things you can do is to make an appointment at the adolescent clinic of the nearest children's hospital. Adolescent clinics are set up to deal with physical problems as well as worries and fears. A younger teenager will probably need to go with a parent; older adolescents may prefer to go alone. Medical centers may also have specialty clinics or eating disorder out-patient and inpatient units. You may have a teen clinic in your high school. If not, you may be able to get help from the school nurse or a counselor. For college students the health service can be a valuable resource.

Not every area is large enough to have a children's hospital or medical center. Maybe your town is small and has only a family doctor. Start with him or her. In large cities consult the Yellow Pages under "Physicians and Surgeons." Or check the listings under psychological, social work, or mental health services. Another resource is the county medical society. Finally, the national eating disorder organizations listed in Chapter 12 can be extremely useful.

Check out these resources with friends, relatives, or your family doctor. That way you're more likely to end up with someone who has proven skill in working with eating disorders.

Above all, you should feel comfortable with your doctor or therapist and believe that the two of you can work together toward your common goal. Remember that eating disorders have no one cause and no one cure. Often a combination of approaches is necessary, and that takes time. Don't expect an instant cure, and don't use an organization or therapist who promises a cure in exchange for lots of money.

How Much Will It Cost?

Treatment for an eating disorder may be expensive, but in the long run the complications of an untreated eating disorder may be even more expensive. Find out if your family's health insurance will cover some of the costs. If money is a problem, doctors and therapists sometimes set up payment plans or use a sliding scale of fees. Be sure you understand the payment plan and the details of treatment before you start. If the cost is more than you can afford, look into state and county mental health facilities. Sometimes churches provide free pastoral counseling, and many eating disorder support groups are free.

Individual Therapy

Individual psychotherapy is one-to-one counseling. Often it is a good way to begin. Meeting with one person seems somehow less scary than meeting with a whole group of people. Nevertheless, the prospect of revealing one's innermost thoughts and feelings to a stranger can be threatening to some people. It is natural to feel nervous when you start with a therapist. Remember that a therapist must maintain confidentiality; that means that whatever you say stays in the room or in the hospital.

The methods of individual therapy are as different as the therapists themselves. Many therapists invite you to meet with them for a get-acquainted visit (sometimes at no charge). At that time they can tell you their credentials and ways of working, and you can ask questions. The American Anorexia/Bulimia Association will provide you with a list of questions you can ask a therapist. AABA suggests questions that fall into three categories. The first, the background of the therapist, includes such questions as "What is your training?" and "How many clients with eating disorders do you see?" The second set of questions has to do with the process of change. For example, you might want to ask how much your family will be involved and if the therapist uses medication or hospitalization. The last category covers "nuts and bolts" issues such as frequency of sessions, length of sessions, and mode of payment.

Some therapists are "directive"; that is, they tell you what they think you should do about your problems. Other therapists are "nondirective," preferring mainly to listen to you, help you examine treatment alternatives, and let you decide what to do. Some therapists share parts of their own lives with their clients; others do no sharing and want no questions about themselves.

You may find after a reasonable trial period (several visits or less) that you don't like a particular therapist's way of working. You are not obligated to stay with a therapist you don't like. But be sure not to use that as an excuse for stopping therapy entirely. There are plenty of other therapists.

You need to be completely honest with your therapist. Give progress a chance by helping in every way. Remember, it is not your job to make the therapist like you. Your job as a client is to find ways (with the help of the therapist) to change and get better.

Most therapists make a contract, either verbal or written, with the client covering the issues they want to work on together. A contract keeps both client and therapist focused. Why are you there? What do you want to accomplish? The most useful individual therapy addresses the eating disorder behaviors (i.e., bingeing, purging, starving) as well as their underlying causes. Therapists can help with issues of self-esteem, control, and stress as well as anxiety and depression. Individual sessions usually last for about fifty minutes, once a week.

Starting therapy is scary, but once you have made the decision to begin, you'll feel relieved. On the other hand, don't expect an instant cure. Getting better will be hard work but worth the effort.

Group Therapy

Making the decision to begin group therapy may be even harder, but your therapist can probably help you. Your therapist may suggest that you participate in a group in addition to individual sessions. There is usually a set fee for such a group, which is led by a professional. The group may meet in the therapist's office, in a clinic, or in a hospital. Participants benefit from the experiences of other members who face similar problems. An advantage of being in a group is that you do not have to do all the talking. You will undoubtedly learn from others and feel supported by them. If you behave in certain dysfunctional ways with other people and/or with food, one of the group members is sure to point that out to you. Because group stability is important, the leader will expect regular attendance. Therapy groups usually meet once a week for an hour or longer.

Support Groups

Support groups, which are often called self-help groups, are more informal and may be organized by people affected by a certain condition. They are not meant as a substitute for professional help. Rather, they are meant as a *supplement* to medical or mental health services, a way for the person with an eating disorder (and somtimes her family) to obtain additional help.

Self-help/support groups, which are often free, may meet in churches, schools, or community centers. Leaders of these groups are not necessarily professionals; the facilitator may be someone who has herself recovered from an eating disorder. Regular attendance is useful but not mandatory.

A support group may be organized for a certain condition, such as anorexia or bulimia. The best group for you is one that addresses your particular issue. If possible, try different groups until you find the one that works best for you. Many of the national eating disorder organizations listed in Chapter 12 sponsor self-help/support groups.

Family Therapy

In Chapter 4 we discussed the family's possible role in the development of an eating disorder. Families can also play an important part in a person's recovery from an eating disorder.

Whether living at home or living independently, the person with the disorder is almost always a part of a family. Some families reject family therapy because it seems too much trouble to bring together what could be a big group (parents, brothers, sisters, even grandparents). Besides that, other family members may say, "She's the sick one; we're not." Specialists learned long ago, however, that when one person in a family is having trouble, others are probably in trouble too. The whole family may be able to benefit from help whether or not they realize it or will admit it.

Satir compares the family to a mobile. A mobile balances by the shortening and lengthening of the strings or by the rearrangement of the distances between the pieces. The situation is similar to a family in which each person is in a different stage of development. When one person changes, the rest of the family members must also change. Therefore, the goal of family therapy in the case of an eating disorder is to change the behavior of everyone in the family, not just the person with the disorder.

Family therapy may be slow and painstaking, but it is likely to be well worth the trouble. In the first place, not all members of the family have to attend every time. Sometimes the therapist may ask all of the siblings to come without the parents. At another time, the therapist may invite only the parents. Or the parents and therapist may meet with the person who has the eating disorder.

Family members may be too closely connected (or not connected enough); they may not know how to laugh and enjoy each other; they may be hiding family "secrets"; or their expectations may be too high or unrealistic. Or they may simply need help in changing their communication patterns, the ways they habitually talk (or don't talk) within the family.

In some cases the family therapist may recommend hospitalization for a client.

Will I Have to Go to a Hospital?

Hospitalization is most often used when other forms of help have failed. A doctor may suggest hospitalization because of a person's weight loss or depression or both. Such a person may be so starved or so depressed that her life is threatened.

Another reason for hospitalization is to establish new and healthier patterns of behavior without outside interference. A person who does well in the hospital should realize the need for *more* help rather than less when she is again living in the real world with all of society's demands. Hospitalization is a major interruption in a person's life, however, and is suggested only after much thought and discussion. If your doctor suggests hospitalization, taking a tour of the facility in advance may help to relieve your anxiety and make you more comfortable with the idea.

Rachel Revisited

Remember Rachel McCarthy who had a problem with bulimia? Rachel reports that the most helpful person for her was the psychiatrist she saw as a college freshman. Under his guidance she entered a hospital program for people with eating disorders. There she learned how to take control of her life, including her eating, how to change her thoughts, and how to live more for herself than for anyone else, especially her family. Rachel says,

"In the hospital they used cognitive restructuring, and they taught me relaxation techniques. I was able to return to school six months later. I still had occasional bouts of bingeing and purging after that. Since about four years ago, I haven't had a problem with food. However, the issues of control, perfectionism, 'shoulds,' worrying about how I will be perceived by people I care about, and getting the most out of life—all these things continue. Lately, I've been under some stress, but the bulimia hasn't returned. I feel much better about myself, and I try to deal with the feelings rather than numbing them out. Occasionally, I see a counselor for help."

Medication

Wouldn't it be nice if a person with an eating disorder could swallow a pill and suddenly get better? Maybe, maybe not. One disadvantage would be that the person would miss a valuable chance for self-understanding. People who have been involved in individual, group, or family therapy usually have learned much about themselves and others in the process. They have wrestled with their inner demons and, as a result, have become stronger.

Often medication is not necessary in the treatment of eating disorders. Beware of anyone who promises a miracle cure as the result of a supplement or medicine that has not been scientifically tested. Medications don't usually help much in the treatment of anorexia nervosa. Research goes on. Up to now, the most promising results have been with antidepressants in the treatment of bulimia. Whether or not the person is actually depressed, this group of medications seems to help. Exactly which antidepressant to use will be up to you and your doctor. Other medications are currently being used to reduce depression in compulsive eaters.

In any case, a psychiatrist who specializes in eating disorders should be the one to prescribe such medications, which can sometimes have unpleasant side effects.

Many people with eating disorders find that a combination of therapies works best for them.

Jenny: Success!

"I can't say that any one thing was most helpful. There were several things—individual and group therapy, twelve-step support groups, and nutrition counseling. I have found changes in lifestyle, friendships, spirituality, and acceptance of self through four years of recovery. My fears of food have decreased, my obsessive behavior with the scale has lessened. My knowledge and acceptance of the disease have improved steadily. My recovery [from bulimia] began when I admitted I had a problem. My abstinence depends on a balance between my emotions, my physical well-being, and my spiritual involvement. If I'm afraid or angry, I can often slip back into bingeing and purging. I try to keep in touch with friends in recovery on a regular basis. I journal my feelings, structure my time, and read literature related to recovery."

Now What?

Eventually, a person with an eating disorder reaches the point of taking (or retaking) control of her own life. She decides how much she is comfortable weighing, how much she should eat, and how much to exercise. Taking control is a good feeling, but it is also scary. A nutrition counselor can be a great help during this phase.

Seemingly simple activities such as choosing new clothes may be difficult. A person who is used to being to skinny may feel "fat" when she has gained some weight and her clothes seem too tight. A person who thinks she's too fat may buy clothes so small that she has trouble getting into them. She may buy shapeless garments that look like last summer's camping tent. Or she may refuse to buy clothes at all. And yet buying new outfits of appropriate size may be just the thing to give her self-esteem a boost.

Eating at friends' houses or restaurants or going to parties may be another challenge. A support person such as an OA sponsor can help the person over such hurdles.

Remember that recovery is a process that takes time.

Don't expect too much of yourself or anyone you know with an eating disorder. One mistake, one slip, or one step backward is not the end of the world. Everyone makes mistake; everyone fails at times. Being able to accept and live with failure is one trait of a mentally healthy person.

Give yourself time and space to explore life, to find out who you are and where you're going. Don't expect too much of yourself. No one ever reaches perfection.

Also, *getting* better doesn't necessarily mean *feeling* better. As you recover, you'll begin to face your problems head-on instead of hiding out with food or diets. In the past you may have binged as a way of dealing with anxiety and uncomfortable feelings. Now you are tolerating those feelings and finding more healthy ways to deal with them. That can be uncomfortable.

Don't be impatient if your eating disorder continues for a while after you start therapy. That is not unusual. Don't be surprised if things even get *worse* for a time before they get better. This difficult period means that you are now dealing with feelings that you formerly numbed out with food or the absence of food.

Recovery means learning to trust again—others, as well as yourself. The more you become involved in life, the more support you need from others. Compare yourself only to yourself, not to other people or to some ideal. Forget that old "ideal" body image and be yourself.

You will learn that although you have stopped destructive eating behaviors, life still has its problems. You can deal with problems. Life's challenges make living fun.

CHAPTER 10

Recognizing an Eating Disorder

I s there anyone in this country who has never tried to diet? On the other hand, everyone has eaten too much at one time or another. Remember the time you "binged" on Halloween candy? What about last year's Thanksgiving dinner? How about Cousin Ozzie's wedding in June? You didn't eat a thing all day and then "pigged out" at the reception.

A person involved in such eating-related situations wouldn't say she was eating-disordered. How do we recognize an eating disorder when we see it? Or what if we don't really see it, but suspect it? What if the person you're worried about is you? What can we do about the person who refuses to admit that she has an eating disorder?

Maggie took a long time recognizing her own problem behavior. She read an article in a women's magazine about eating disorders. The article scared her so much that she denied it described her. "My pattern was to purge after meals either when I was alone or when I went to my parents' house. My anorexic behavior started after a severe depression at age twently-five. I lost twenty pounds in a month and then was afraid to resume normal eating, but it never occurred to me that I had an eating disorder."

Fifteen-year-old Tina says her anorexia began two years ago, but she just thought of it as dieting until her mother began calling her a "jumping bean" and commenting on her low weight.

How Can You Tell?

The following lists may help you recognize an eating disorder in yourself or someone you know. Despite the separate categories for each condition, many of the characteristics overlap. Did you know that a person can be both anorexic and bulimic? What about the person who eats only three peas for lunch and then vomits them?

A person with anorexia nervosa probably has some of the following characteristics:

- Shows extreme weight loss
- Wears bulky clothes to conceal weight loss
- Fears getting fat and continues to diet
- Shows unusual behaviors related to food, such as preparing it for others while eating next to nothing herself
- Avoids situations where food is served
- Engages in excessive exercise or hyperactivity (*i.e.*, is constantly "on the move")
- Has spells of dizziness or fainting, feels cold, looks pale
- Experiences stopping of menstrual periods
- Has perfectionistic tendencies

• Loses hair
• Has growth of fine hair on body.

A person with bulimia may exhibit:

• Preoccupation with food and weight
• Sore, red knuckles from induced vomiting
• Tooth decay
• Sore throat
• Puffy face, bloodshot eyes, swollen glands ("chip-munk cheeks")
• Weight fluctuations
• Mood swings
• Excessive need for approval and praise
• Self-criticism
• Abuse of alcohol or drugs; stealing.

Compulsive eaters exhibit all or some of these behaviors:

• Constant dieting and talking about weight while at the same time gaining weight
• A social life that revolves around food, or the absence of social life because of concerns about weight and food
• Bingeing or eating too little in public
• Avoidance of activities such as physical education or sports because of concern about weight
• Fantasies and talk about how good life will be when the person "gets thin."

Compulsive exercisers share some of these characteristics:

• Devote several hours every day to exercising

- Think of themselves as worthy only when they get "enough" exercise
- Never get enough exercise.

If the person with some of these signs and symptoms is you, the best thing to do is get help. Go to someone you trust (it doesn't have to be your parents) and tell your story.

Denial

What do we do when a person refuses to admit that she has an eating disorder? You as a friend are obligated to say something. With careful consideration, you can make that task easier for both of you.

Give some thought to the time and place you'll express your concerns. You already know the person has problems with food. A dinner date might not provide optimum circumstances. How about a nonfood occasion, such as a walk, when you could give her a list of resources for help. Although she may not seem interested at the time, your friend might decide to use your list later.

Another good way to express your caring is through the use of "I" messages. "I" messages state *your* problem with the behavior. Such messages require careful thought because most of us are not used to giving them. Unless we're careful, they may come out as "you" messages, which can put the other person on the defensive.

Here is an example of an attempt that came out a bit garbled. "I'm concerned that you don't look well, that you look too thin." The message started out as an "I" message but ended up as a "you" message. The person is likely to answer: "I'm *not* too thin. Why don't you mind your own business?"

Try this one: "I'm missing the good times we used to have together. I'm concerned. Is there anything I can do to help?" In this message the speaker gets across her caring without seeming to put the other person down. Keep in mind that your friend is a *person*, not an eating disorder. Try to find qualities about her that make her special apart from her problem.

Getting Ready

The authors of *Surviving an Eating Disorder* suggest seven guidelines for talking with a person you are concerned about. First, speak to your friend before going to her parents. You don't want to jeopardize her trust in you by "going over her head." Second, pick a time to talk to your friend when you are feeling calm, not when you're angry or hurt. Remember that you want to avoid putting the other person on the defensive. Third, pick a time when you know you both have time and won't be interrupted. Fourth, consider writing down ahead of time what you want to say. You want to be sure to include what you're concerned about, how you feel ("I" messages), and your goals for this discussion. Remember that you cannot get someone to stop bingeing, purging, or starving. That has to be the person's own choice. Fifth, practice the discussion with someone you know who is also aware of the problem, or practice alone. Sixth, if the discussion seems to be getting out of hand, stop for a while. Tell the person you can continue when both of you are more calm. Finally, if you believe the problem has reached a state of emergency, tell your friend that you're going to have to get help now—because you care.

Nancy: Maybe She's Right

Says Nancy, "It makes me furious that Mom told her friend she thought I was sick because of my 'irregular habits.' She said I only eat peanuts. I guess she's kind of right. (I know she's right.) Maybe that's what makes me so mad. Well, I'll keep working on it."

Although it's hard for Nancy to admit that she has a problem, she is showing a crack in her defenses. When Nancy's mother spoke the truth, Nancy wasn't at all pleased. She did, however, think about her mother's words. A few days later she decided to get help.

Being a Friend/Having a Friend

If you are a friend of a person with an eating disorder, don't underestimate your importance. On the other hand, if *you* are the person with the eating disorder, don't underrate the importance of good friendships. One family therapist says that he has learned the importance of friends over the years. Sometimes when confronted with a serious problem of his own, he goes to friends for advice. Friends not only provide a listening ear but often give good advice. Sometimes, however, friends are not available. Then, says the family therapist, he supplements the missing help with help from *his* therapist.

In spite of all your efforts, your eating-disordered friend may still seem to want to do nothing. Chances are, though, she'll give your words some thought. At least the secret is out of the bag, out in the open where she has the best chance of doing something about it—when and if she chooses to do so.

CHAPTER 11

Prevention

K nowing that eating disorders have become a national epidemic, what can you do to prevent the spread?

The first thing you can do is to learn the facts. If you have read this book and any of the others listed in the back of the book, you've gone a long way in helping to dispel the myths. Learning the facts surrounding weight and our culture's hangups about weight is most important. You are the first line of resistance in the fight against eating disorders. Here are some guidelines:

- Don't hand down misinformation to the next generation or pass it along to friends. You have the facts; let diet and food myths stop with you.
- Avoid making comments about other people's shapes and sizes. Remember, the body is only a wrapping for the valuable person inside.
- Never tell a person to lose weight. Only the person herself can decide how much she wants to weigh.

Second, don't diet. What you're after is a lifetime eating plan. To be really healthy, eat five or more servings of fruits and vegetables a day. Keep salt and fats low, but allow yourself some fun foods too. That way you won't be tempted to binge. In general, eat only when you're hungry.

If you begin to think about dieting, ask yourself why. Maybe you're not really dealing with food issues; maybe you need to talk to someone about feelings. Learn to feel your feelings (even the negative ones), to express them, and to share them with someone who cares about you. Talking to a counselor or therapist may help you to sort out important emotions before an eating disorder starts. If someone says you need to lose weight, consult a medical doctor or nutrition specialist before doing anything else. Remember, people who go on diets unlearn the body's natural hunger and satisfaction signals.

Third, care about yourself. Remember you are, and should be, your own best friend.

- Love yourself. You are unique, one of a kind. Don't destroy yourself by treating yourself badly.
- Don't forget that you were not put on this earth to please others. Please yourself; learn to believe in yourself. How you live is *your* choice.
- Your body is yours. Love it. Realize that bumps and bulges are part of a developing woman's figure. That's you, a developing woman. Men, too, can have a little fat. Don't be afraid to be normal.
- Don't expect too much of yourself or others. You're young. You have much to learn and plenty of time to learn it. Everyone makes mistakes. Nobody's perfect.
- Try to take control of your life in ways other than deciding what to eat. For example, don't let your parents do things for you that you are capable of

doing for yourself. Maybe you need to get a job and feel good about making your own money.

• Don't be a couch potato. Try to get at least thirty minutes of enjoyable exercise three times a week. Walking and swimming are wonderful, but choose whatever turns you on. Dancing? Biking? Soccer? Gymnastics? Volleyball? Badminton? Have fun doing *something*. Get up and get your blood circulating.

• Buy yourself some new clothes that fit you just as you are right now.

• Go to your favorite restaurant with family or friends. Eat and enjoy.

Fourth, trust yourself.

• Don't believe everything you read in magazines or see on TV. Realize that the very people admired for their sleek bodies may themselves be eating disorder victims.

• Get a black marker and put an X through magazine and newspaper ads that promote negative stereotypes about weight, food, or body image.

• If you hear or see advertisements degrading to women, call or write a letter of protest.

• Your parents are undoubtedly wonderful people, but they don't know everything. Parents are the result of a combination of the right and wrong parenting of *their* parents and so on back to the beginning of time. Parents almost always want what is best for their children, but they don't always know the best way of getting it. As a soon-to-be-adult, you eventually have to decide what's best for you. Of course, you don't know everything either.

Listen to what your parents and other important adults have to say. Then decide.

Fifth, make an effort to have good friends and spend time with them, but don't believe everything *they* tell you either. Realize that your friends are under pressure too—from their parents, from the media, and from society. Your friends may know less than you do about what's good for them or for you. You may have to be the one to lead the way to healthier, happier living.

CHAPTER 12

Resources

National Referral and Self-Help Organizations

These organizations offer a range of services plus (in some cases) names of doctors, counselors, outpatient facilities, hospitals, and support groups. All provide information about their services, either free or at a nominal charge to cover the costs of printing and mailing. You can either phone or write for information.

> The American Anorexia/Bulimia Association, Inc. (AABA)
> c/o Regent Hospital
> 425 East 61st Street
> New York, NY 10021
> (212) 891-8686

The AABA has been in existence since 1978; membership is open to all. This is a tax-exempt, nonprofit organization. The association believes eating disorders are psychological problems but does not endorse any one treatment. The AABA will send a packet of information on request and appreciates donations.

Anorexia Bulimia Care, Inc. (ABC)
545 Concord Avenue
Cambridge, MA 02138
(617) 492-7670

ABC is a nonprofit organization of professionals, family members, those with eating disorders, and other concerned persons. It provides referrals through a registry of professionals, which includes the providers' treatment philosophy and the types of insurance they accept. The organization also publishes a quarterly newsletter. Members receive discounts on services, film rentals, and admission to an annual conference. College students may apply for internships. A crisis hotline operates from 9 a.m. to 6 p.m. Call (617) 492-7670.

National Association of Anorexia Nervosa and Associated Disorders (ANAD)
P.O. Box 7
Highland Park, IL 60035
(708) 831-3438

Founded in 1976, ANAD was the first national nonprofit educational and self-help organization in America dedicated to alleviating eating disorders. ANAD offers many services (all free), including counseling, information, referrals, self-help groups for victims and parents, educational programs, and listings of therapists, hospitals, and clinics. It supports and encourages research. ANAD answers personal letters and operates a hotline (708) 831-3438. Other programs and services include a newsletter, consumer protection, and help in fighting insurance discrimination.

Anorexia Nervosa and Related Eating Disorders, Inc.
(ANRED)
P.O. Box 5102
Eugene, OR 97405
(503) 344-1144

ANRED is a national nonprofit organization that collects
and distributes information about eating and exercise
disorders. The organization also sponsors workshops,
provides speakers, and gives training to mental health
professionals who work with clients who have eating
disorders.

National Eating Disorders Organization (NEDO)
445 East Granville Road
Worthington, OH 43085
(614) 436-1112

NEDO publishes a quarterly newsletter, a bibliog-
raphy, and information about eating disorders. It also
offers free support groups, maintains an international
referral list of professionals, and sponsors a national conference every fall. The NEDO hotline, operating Mondays
through Fridays, is (614) 436-1112.

Twelve-Step Self-Help ₁

Overeaters Anonymous (OA)
P.O. Box 44020
Rio Rancho, NM 87174
(505) 891-2664

OA is a special kind of self-help group, international in
scope, and modeled after the program of Alcoholics

Anonymous. Participants share a preoccupation with food that has interfered with their lives. OA has no membership dues; it is self-supporting through contributions. It is based on the premise of abstinence, which each member defines for himself or herself. Other tools of recovery are attendance at meetings, use of the telephone for support, reading of literature, writing about feelings, anonymity, service, and sponsorship (someone to call for help).

Food Addiction

National Food Addiction Hotline
1-800-USA-0088

Callers to this number receive counselor referrals, referrals to Overeaters Anonymous groups, a confidential food addiction questionnaire, and free literature on food addiction. The hotline is associated with the Florida Institute of Technology, School of Psychology, 150 West University Boulevard, Melbourne, FL 32901. (407) 768-8000, extension 8104.

Epilogue

Remember Liz from the beginning of this book? Her story has a happy ending. She decided to take her mother's first suggestion and went to therapy on her own at the college health center. Later her family got involved. Since then, Liz's life has not been without struggles. She still wrestles with others' opinions of her; she wants everyone to like her. Her eating patterns will probably never be what other people consider "normal." She keeps her weight below average, exercises more than most, and still looks at her slender thighs with horror. ("They're so fat.") Now at age twenty-eight, however, Liz has a ready smile that comes from being happy (most of the time). She teaches in a preschool and has her own apartment. She's engaged to a guy who knows almost everything about her past but loves her unconditionally. Most important of all, Liz has finally learned to love herself.

Glossary

addiction Physical or psychological dependence on a substance.

assertiveness The ability to get one's own needs met in healthy ways.

anorexia nervosa Disorder that causes great weight loss in people preoccupied with dieting and getting excessively thin.

binge eating disorder Condition involving uncontrolled eating, sometimes in secret.

bingeing (sometimes spelled "binging") Eating a large amount of food in a short time.

bulimia nervosa Frequent episodes of binge eating usually followed by purging and feelings of guilt and shame.

codependence Relying on another person or substance (e.g., food) to meet one's needs.

compulsion Irresistible impulse to act regardless of the rationality of the motivation.

diuretic Medication prescribed for cardiac patients to reduce water retention.

dysfunctional Not working properly.

emetic Medication that causes vomiting.

osteoporosis Loss of bone mass and bone minerals, usually occurring in older women.

purging Trying to rid oneself of calories by unnatural means such as vomiting or laxative abuse.

setpoint theory The belief that everyone has a genetically determined body weight.

yo yo syndrome Extremes of weight fluctuation over a period of time in spite of, or perhaps because of, dieting.

For Further Reading

Abraham, Suzanne, and Llewellyn-Jones, Derek. *Eating Disorders: The Facts*. Oxford University Press, 1987.

Bradshaw, John. *Bradshaw On: The Family*. Pompano Beach, FL: Health Communications, Inc., 1988.

Brownell, Kelly, and Foreyt, John. *Handbook of Eating Disorders*. New York: Basic Books, 1986.

Bruch, Hilde. *The Golden Cage: The Enigma of Anorexia Nervosa*. Cambridge: Harvard University Press, 1978.

Cauwels, Janice. *Bulimia: The Binge Purge Compulsion*. Garden City, NY: Doubleday, 1983.

Chernin, Kim. *The Hungry Self: Women, Eating, and Identity*. New York: Harper & Row, 1985.

Dowling, Colette. *You Mean I Don't Have to Feel This Way?: New Help for Depression, Anxiety, and Addiction*. New York: Scribner's, 1991.

Foreyt, John, and Goodrick, G. Ken. *Living Without Dieting*. Houston, TX: Harrison Publishing, 1992.

Garner, David, and Garfinkel, Paul. *Handbook of Psychotherapy for Anorexia and Bulimia*. New York: Guilford Press, 1985.

Hall, Lindsey, and Cohn, Leigh. *Eating Without Fear*. New York: Bantam Books, 1990.

Hendricks, Gay. *Learning to Love Yourself: A Guide to Becoming Centered*. New York: Prentice Hall Press, 1987.

Hollis, Judi. *Fat Is a Family Affair*. New York: Harper & Row, 1985.

Hutchinson, Marcia. *Transforming Body Image*. Trumansburg, NY: Crossing Press, 1985.

Jeffers, Susan. *Feel the Fear and Do It Anyway.* New York: Harcourt Brace Jovanovich, 1987.

Kano, Susan. *Making Peace With Food.* New York: Harper & Row, 1989.

Kinoy, Barbara; Miller, Estelle; and Atchley, John. *When Will We Laugh Again?: Living and Dealing with Anorexia Nervosa and Bulimia.* New York: Columbia University Press, 1984.

Landau, Elaine. *Why Are They Starving Themselves?* New York: Julian Messner, 1983.

Larocca, Felix, ed. *Eating Disorders.* San Francisco: Jossey-Bass, Inc., 1986.

Levenstein, Harvey. *Revolution at the Table: The Transformation of the American Diet.* New York: Oxford University Press, 1988.

McLuhan, Marshall, and Fiore, Quentin. *The Medium Is the Massage.* New York: Random House, 1967.

Mellody, Pia. *Facing Codependence.* New York: Harper & Row, 1989.

Meyer, Ken. *Real Women Don't Diet!* Silver Spring, MD: Bartleby Press, 1993.

Minuchin, Salvador; Rosman, Bernice; and Baker, Lester. *Psychosomatic Families.* Cambridge: Harvard University Press, 1978.

O'Neill, Cherry. *Starving for Attention.* New York: Dell Publishing Co., Inc., 1982.

Orbach, Susie. *Fat Is a Feminist Issue.* New York: Berkley Books, 1979.

———. *Fat Is a Feminist Issue II.* New York: Berkley Books, 1982.

Roth, Geneen. *Feeding the Hungry Heart: The Experience of Compulsive Eating.* Bobbs-Merrill Co., 1984.

———. *Breaking Free from Compulsive Eating.* New York: Bobbs-Merrill Co., 1986.

———. *When Food Is Love: Exploring the Relationship Between Eating and Intimacy.* New York: Dutton, 1991.

Kayley C.

Root, Maria; Fallon, Patricia; and Friedrich, William. *Bulimia: A Systems Approach to Treatment.* New York: W.W. Norton & Company, 1986.

Sandbek, Terence. *The Deadly Diet: Recovering from Anorexia and Bulimia.* Oakland, CA: New Harbinger Publications, Inc., 1986.

Satir, Virginia. *Peoplemaking.* Palo Alto, CA: Science and Behavior Books, 1972.

————. *Meditations and Inspirations.* Berkeley, CA: Celestial Arts, 1985.

Siegel, Michele; Brisman, Judith; and Weinshel, Margot. *Surviving an Eating Disorder: New Perspectives for Family and Friends.* New York: Harper & Row, 1988.

Stein, Particia, and Unell, Barbara. *Anorexia Nervosa: Finding the Lifeline.* Minneapolis: CompCare Publishers, 1986.

Stierlin, Helm, and Weber, Gunthard. *Unlocking the Family Door: A Systemic Approach to the Understanding and Treatment of Anorexia Nervosa.* New York: Brunner/Mazel, 1989.

Stinnett, Nick, and De Frain, John. *Secrets of Strong Families.* Boston: Little, Brown and Company, 1985.

Valette, Brett. *A Parent's Guide to Eating Disorders.* New York: Walker Publishing Company, 1985.

Wegscheider-Cruse, Sharon. *Another Chance.* Palo Alto, CA: Science and Behavior Books, Inc., 1989.

Whitfield, Charles. *Healing the Child Within.* Deerfield Beach, FL: Health Communications, 1987.

Index

A

abstinence, 108
abuse, child, 7, 63, 78–79
addiction, 6, 8, 70–71, 90, 93, 104
   from compulsion, 94, 96
advertising, as thought control, 22
affirmations, 106
alcohol, 39, 51, 58, 70
alcoholic, 6, 46, 48, 61, 67–68, 108
Alcoholics Anonymous, 57, 92, 101
American Anorexia/Bulimia Association (AABA), 117–118, 136
Anderson, Christopher, 23
anger, 43
   expressing, 13, 32, 59
   failure to express, 44
   using constructively, 33, 59
anorexia nervosa, 2, 3, 4, 9–15, 13, 16, 20, 26, 30, 35, 46, 51, 57, 60, 67, 73, 76, 81, 85, 88–90, 92, 94, 101, 107, 120, 123
   becoming bulimia, 97–99
   characteristics of, 9–10, 93, 127–128
   deaths from 57, 89, 90

Anorexia Nervosa and Related Eating Disorders, Inc., 3, 138
antidepressants, 123
anxiety, unhealthy, 59, 67
appreciation, family, 52, 53
assertiveness, 13, 32, 64
   training, 37

B

behavior
   addictive, 6
   compulsive, 7, 58
   coping, 3
   self-destructive, 11–12, 59, 70, 90, 104
   replacing, 105
beliefs, challenging, 73
Bepko, Claudia, 7
binge eating disorder (BED), 14–16
bingeing, 12, 13, 42, 67, 79, 85–86, 96
binge-purge cycle, 47, 93, 104
body
   attitude toward, 74
   image, 9, 92, 125
   weight, 9, 12
boundaries, 77–78
   lack of, 69
Bradshaw, John, 43, 58, 69, 81

*Breaking Free from Compulsive
     Eating*, 110
Bruch, Hilde, 17
Bruno, Barbara Altman, 107
Brush, Stephanie, 35–36
bulimia nervosa, 3, 4, 6, 12–14,
     16, 20, 23, 30, 47, 51, 55,
     57, 58, 60, 61, 64, 67, 73,
     76, 77, 78, 81, 85, 92, 94,
     100–101, 108, 120, 122,
     123
   characteristics of, 93–94, 128
   deaths from 57, 90

C
caregiver, mother as, 39, 77, 79
Carpenter, Karen, 24, 25
change, taking risk of, 80
children, concerned with
     weight, 4, 35
child within, 58
Citizen Jane, 23
clinic, adolescent, 116
codependent, 61, 63, 69, 96
commitment, family, 52, 53
communication, family, 10
compulsive eater, 3, 14–16, 50,
     59, 60, 62, 67, 76, 79, 94,
     101, 105, 108, 123
   characteristics of, 16, 128
compulsions, 7, 8, 93
   multiple, 92, 96
control
   excessive, 9
   lack of, 10
   loss of, 14, 47, 93
   problems with, 6, 122
   taking (back), 10, 37, 46, 124
coping ability, family, 52, 53

D
Deadly Diet, The, 56
De Frain, John, 52–53
denial, 129–130
depression, 6, 12, 15, 32, 39, 56,
     93–94, 123
diet, 4, 10, 15, 16, 19–21, 24,
     21, 24, 31, 43, 82,
     132–137
   as a business, 26, 83
   crash, 35
   harm from, 25, 36, 85
   pills, 16
diuretics, 12, 16, 86

E
eating disorder, 32, 56, 80, 101
   and age, 5
   death from, 24, 57
   and gender, 5–6
   recognizing, 126–131
   and social classes, 4–5
Eating Without Fear, 100
emetics, 86–87
emotions, destructive, 47, 55, 56
enabler, 48, 54
exercise, 2, 3, 36, 76, 83–84
   compulsive, 16, 128–129
   excessive, 12

F
failure, feelings of, 42–43
families, 38–54
   dysfunctional, 48
Fat Is a Family Affair, 61, 94
Fat Is a Feminist Issue, 31
fear
   of adulthood, 39
   of fatness, 9

of food, 60, 67, 83
Feeding the Hungry Heart, 107
feelings
  expressing, 13, 33, 66, 69, 133
  feeling your, 55–68, 133
  inability to express, 31, 41
  loving, 74
  negative, 13
  painful, 7
  sexual, 43, 74–75
Feel the Fear and Do It Anyway,
    61
female athlete triad, 16–17
Fonda, Jane, 23
food, "good" vs. "bad,"
    109–110, 112
friend with eating disorder,
    helping, 129–131

G
Garner, David, 27–28
genetic link, 38–39, 43, 46
Gilbert Pierce, Donna, 92, 93
growing up
  coping with, 80–81
  fear of, 39
guilt, 12, 21, 32, 57

H
hair
  body, 90
  facial, 30
Hall, Lindsey, 100–101
Handbook of Eating Disorders,
    84
helplessness, 58
help, seeking, 115–116
Hendricks, Gay, 66, 70–71
Hendricks, Kathryn, 70–71

Henrich, Christy, 57
hero/heroine, family, 47, 48, 49
high, addictive, 93
high pot/low pot, 70
Hollis, Judi, 61, 94
hospitalization, 89, 121–122

I
intimacy, problems with, 6, 10

J
Jeffers, Susan, 61
journal, keeping, 112

K
Keys, Ancel, 97–99

L
laxatives, 12, 16, 47, 86
Learning to Love Yourself, 66
Levenstein, Harvey, 27
Lewis, Karen, 51–52
loneliness, 56, 67
lost child, family, 48–49
love, 59
  need for, 12
  shown in worry, 45

M
mascot, family, 48–49, 50
McLuhan, Marshall, 26
medication, 123
meditation, 113–114
Meditations and Inspirations,
    113
Medium Is the Massage, The, 26
Mellody, Pia, 69
men, eating disorders in, 5–6
menstrual period, 9, 16, 30, 91

messages
    family, 70
    media, 4, 19–25
    self-, 105–106
    sibling, 50–51
Murray, John, 21
myths, eating disorder, 4–6

N
Narcotics Anonymous, 92
National Association of Anorexia
    and Associated Disorders
    (ANAD), 26, 137
National Association to Advance
    Fat Acceptance
    (NAAFA), 107
needs, meeting one's own, 61,
    62, 69
nicotine, 7, 58
numbness, feelings of, 6, 50, 66
nutrition plan, 107–108

O
O'Neill,Cherry Boone, 23–24
Orbach, Susie, 31
osteoporosis, 17, 23
Overeaters Anonymous, 57, 58,
    60, 75, 80, 92, 101, 108,
    138
overprotection, 21, 65
overweight, 2, 15, 34
    as health hazard, 23

P
pain, emotional, 15, 18, 76
parents
    accepting one's, 106
    failing to let go, 42
    feelings about, 66

Peoplemaking, 69–70
people-pleasers, 24, 34
perfectionism, 9, 43, 90, 93,
    113, 122
powerlessness, 80
prevention, eating disorder,
    132–135
pride, in self-starvation, 14
purging, 13, 25, 79, 85–86

R
reality, accepting, 69, 75
recovery, 80, 100–101
relationships
    destructive, 58, 66
    father-daughter, 42
    mother-daughter, 39
    problems with, 94
    undesirable, 12
resentment, 59
Revolution at the Table, 27
role model, mother as, 39
roles, family, 48–50
Roth, Geneen, 107, 110–111
Russell, Lillian, 27

S
sadness, 56
Sandbek, Terence, 56
Satir, Virginia, 69–70, 113,
    120–121
scale, avoiding, 112
scapegoat, family, 48, 49
Secrets of Strong Families,
    52–53
self-awareness, 75
self-esteem, 57, 69–71
    improving, 73–74, 75, 105

low, 6, 13, 21, 37, 45, 49, 70,
    94, 113
self-talk, 105–106
self-worth, 12, 36, 48
setpoint, 83–85, 99
shame, 14, 57, 79
    transfer of, 58
Sheppard, Risa, 25
siblings, 50–52
society
    expectations of, 6, 36
    meaning of fat to, 106–107
starvation, 9, 79, 88, 81
    and infertility, 91–92
Starving for Affection, 23–24
stereotyping, sexual, 65
Stinnett, Nick, 52–53
stress, 13, 15, 113–114, 122
    family, 53
sugar, and bingeing, 109
support group, 36, 50, 60,
    62–63, 73, 80, 93, 102,
    110, 119–120
Surviving an Eating Disorder,
    130

T
Then, Debbie, 28
therapist, 36, 80, 102, 105, 116,
    117–118, 133
therapy
    family, 54, 120–121
    group, 119

individual, 117–118
time, family, 52, 53
treatment
    costs of, 117
    goals of, 104–108
trust
    regaining, 125
    self-, 134
twelve-step program, 57, 59, 80,
    93, 101, 104

U
Upper Limits Problem, 70–71

V
vomiting, 3, 8, 13, 47, 61, 85,
    86–87, 90

W
Wegscheider-Cruse, Sharon,
    67–68
weight loss, 2, 82–83
Weight Watchers, 22, 108
wellness, spiritual, 52, 53
Whitfield, Charles, 58
women
    position in society, 27–37, 79
    strong in connections, 40–41
workaholic, 46

Y
yo-yo syndrome, 16, 107